LOVE AGAIN: A Spiritual Memoir

by Patrick D'Anzel Shaffer
with Sylvester Monroe

RODMAN PUBLIC LIBRARY

```
38212005544496
Main Adult Biography
SHAFFER,   PATRICK    B
S525p
Shaffer, Patrick D'Anzel
Love again : a spiritual
memoir
                 DEC - - 2011
```

Copyright (©) 2011 Patrick D'Anzel Shaffer

All rights reserved.

No part of this publication may be reproduced, stored in a retrieval system, or transmitted in any form or any other means electronic, mechanical, photocopying, recording or otherwise, without the prior written permission of the publisher.

First published by Dog Ear Publishing
4010 W. 86th Street, Ste H
Indianapolis, IN 46268
www.dogearpublishing.net

ISBN: 978-145750-089-3

This book is printed on acid-free paper.

Printed in the United States of America

Praise for *Love Again*

"For those of us who have experienced the reality & pain of divorce, Patrick captures the emotional, spiritual and mental journey toward healing, wholeness and the often evasive joy of reclaiming one's ability to love again. From a man's point of view Patrick puts honest emotion into perspective so that healing can occur. This book is that rare read that balances honesty, vulnerability and transparency; sharing what men don't allow them to say in public. He illustrates for us all that we have the power to 'Begin. End & Love Again'."
~ *Jeff Johnson, MSNBC & the Grio.com Contributor, Author, and TJMS Commentator*

* * * * *

"Patrick Shaffer has mastered his rare gift of blending compassion with truth-telling. Patrick's appeal as an emerging influencer is born of his willingness to be introspective and authentic by sharing his personal challenges and failures for the sake of helping others through his ministry. A charismatic speaker, without question, Patrick stands apart as he openly embraces the tough issues of love and loss — universal concerns with too few ambassadors. Patrick's voice is at once inspiring and necessary."
~ *Tamara Brown, Publisher and Editor-in-Chief of* Urban Influence *magazine*

* * * * *

"LOVE AGAIN is a must-read! Patrick Shaffer is a dynamic voice on the spiritual scene today. His unique perspective on life and love is written in honest reflection and divine revelation."
~ *Bonita Bennett, Publisher and Editor-in-Chief of* Being Single *magazine*

* * * * *

"Patrick hits the nail on the head as he addresses cures for our relationship pain. As men, we often can't express the pain we feel with facing relationship failure, but without taking the steps that Shaffer discusses, our families will continue to suffer. Patrick is putting us back on the right path toward bliss."
~ *Lenny McAllister, political/social commentator and author,* Diary of a Mad Black P.Y.C. *(Proud Young Conservative)*

* * * * *

Acknowledgments

Thank you to my Creator, Sustainer and Lover of my soul Jesus the Christ.

My parents Nash E. and Rosemary E. Shaffer, I live my life fueled by your love and confidence in me. My grandmother Lois, I love you with all my heart. My other grandmother, Cora Murray, thank you and I love you. My siblings Kim, Nash III, Deborah (Brit) and Christopher, I have always felt insulated, covered, and smothered by your love, I love you all very much. Percy Littleton, my Uncle and all my nieces and nephews, I love you! City of Faith Christian Church of Chicago and our Board of Directors, you have been with me every step of the way and I love you for it. Robert and Doris Watson, thank you for letting me be your child, I love you. Jamie (Kathy, Cierra) you have been my best friend for as long as I can remember, thank you very much for that. Elizabeth Lomax (Christine, Brian), I love you! Doreen (god-mother), Spencer Gillespie and the whole family, I love you! My godchildren, Jamie-Nia and Gilbert, god-daddy loves you very much!

Sylvester Monroe, thank you for affirming my words with your keen eye and brilliant mind. I am a better writer because of you. Tamara Brown (Urban Influence), my friend, thank you. Goldie Taylor (Goldie Taylor Brand Communications), you are heaven sent, thank you! LaVenia J. LaVelle, thank you for absolutely everything, your care and concern have made all the difference in the world. I could not have finished this project without you. Regina Brooks, thank you for your help, I appreciate you. Hope Allen, thank you for dignifying my ideas with your sensitivity and expertise. Monique Caradine (Momentum Media Group), thank you for giving me the push I needed at the right moment.

Dr. B. Herbert Martin, Dr. Paul Bishoff, Dr. Ramona Joseph, Dr. John Selders, Dr. Debra Mullen, Dr. Cynthia Lindner, thank you for being a part of my life.

Special thanks to: Toni Judkins, Deborah Olivia Brown, Kiesha Taylor, Marshette Turner, Effie Rolfe, Shelby Wills, Lenny McAlister, Tavis Smiley, Walter W. Whitman and the Soul Children of Chicago (alumni), Emil Wilbekin, Dr. Ronn Elmore, Desiree Rogers, Donald Lawrence, Joel Dreyfuss, David Wilson, Scott Hayes and Altera Web, Daryl Wade and PrakPrint, Cheryl Woodruff, Bonita Bennett, Cliff Kelly.

My friends: Kenneth Curry, Patrick Winfield, Tahir Golden, Michael Washington, Samuel Williams, Anthony Tyler, Ghana Cooper, Daniel Johnson, Aja Carr, Vashawn Mitchell, Joy Challenger, Kenneth Mosley, Lesley Bridges, Faheem Shabazz.

To the many men and women who've left a lasting impression or a faded bruise upon my life, thank you.

Special Thank You

Denae, I wish the love we shared on your parents' porch could have lasted a lifetime. Though life would not let it be so, I thank you for those moonlit nights with me. They will live in my heart forever.

Table of Contents

PREFACE   by Sylvester Monroe ....p. viii

Part One

Chapter I: Take My Breath Away...............................p. 2
Chapter II: Faded Pictures ....p. 11
Chapter III: Lemonade..p. 15
Chapter IV: Dark Victory ....p. 27

Part Two

Chapter V: Changed by the Night ....p. 40
Chapter VI: Rest Well ....p. 44
Chapter VII: When Goodbye is the Last Thing We Say..p. 54
Chapter VIII: Love, No Limit...p. 60

Part Three

Chapter IX: Make Love with Me? ....P. 72
Chapter X: Chest Pains...p. 79
Chapter XI: Reflections in Love ....p. 93
Chapter XII: Love Again ....p. 104

Afterword   Shining on My Face...................................p. 114

*For Devon Jr., Charron Levicy, Jesse Williams, and Jason London,
who are now resting and loving again ...*

Preface

When Patrick and I met to discuss my working on this project, I wasn't at all sure I wanted to do it. Except for a story on interracial marriage and dating I did many years ago, writing about "love" has never been my cup of tea — too mushy, too touchy-feely. But the more we talked the more I realized that the loss of love and loved ones is something everyone deals with sooner or later — regardless of how tough we think we are.

When Patrick called me in late last year, I was still reeling from two devastating losses of my own. My mother had passed unexpectedly in March 2009 almost a year after we buried my father. No matter how much we think we are prepared for such loss, we can never really know just how it will affect us. I knew my father was going to die and I watched him fade away over several months as the lung cancer consumed his life and left him a frail shadow of the man he had been. But when he finally succumbed to the disease, it was not so much sadness I felt, but anger. I was angry because the disease had stolen the father I had longed for all my life as a boy and finally found at the age of 28.

Then not quite a year later, heart disease took the one person in the world I had always been able to depend on. Growing up without my father, my mother had always been not just mother, but father when she had to be, as well as confidant and best friend. She was the person who kept me anchored in the world and I had always wondered what life would be like without her. I had no idea how much it would hurt and how deep and empty a hole it would leave inside me.

I also had no idea how to deal with such loss. That is what this book is all about and ultimately what made me decide to be a part of it. It is said that time heals all wounds. There is much truth in that statement, but what too many of us discover along the way is that it

LOVE AGAIN

takes more than just time. After my first marriage ended, I basically dealt with the loss of my wife's love by delving into my work. Almost immediately after the breakup, I went on the road for nearly 14 straight months covering the 1984 presidential campaign for *Newsweek*. I always thought it was a blessing, because traveling with presidential candidates for 16-hour days, seven days a week left no time to brood about my failed marriage. It also provided a long line of casual "lovers" who passed through my nights like ephemeral dreams, rarely coming even close to touching my still aching heart.

When my second marriage ended 14 years later after nearly seven years, I dealt with that by treating it like I had lost my favorite shirt. One day she was there and the next day she was gone, and I changed nothing in my life except that she was no longer there. I lived in the same big house with the same furniture in the same place and went to work every day just as I had when she was there. As I would have missed my favorite shirt less and less, I no longer missed my wife. Or so I told myself. It wasn't until many years later in counseling that I began to learn how to grieve for the losses of my wives.

As I talked with the doctor about my profound anger and unhappiness after the deaths of my parents and the deep sense of loss I was feeling as I watched the world of journalism that I had loved all my life vanish before my eyes, she said something that made me think about my life in a way I never had before.

"You have never grieved for the loss of (my second wife)," the doctor said.

"But she's not dead!" I snapped back. "We decided to split up, and I moved on."

In fact, what I learned from that therapist is that nothing could have been further from the truth. Indeed, like many people, especially men, I have never dealt with loss at all. I have tried to cheat it by simply ignoring it or tucking it away somewhere out of sight and out of mind. Indeed, I moved on but the debris from that failed marriage and the hole in my soul left from the enormous loss of a woman who had been the love of my life all stayed with me.

Until then I had not fully understood what the marriage counselor meant when she told me I might want to consider psychoanalysis to sort out some of the debris of my life. I told her I had always believed that one should let sleeping dogs lie. "The problem with that," she said, "is that sooner or later they wake up and bite you in the behind."

Whether it is the sleeping dogs of death or marital breakups or beloved way of life, all of us must eventually deal with the loss of people and things we love. Patrick Shaffer's *Love Again* could help put those dogs to rest so we can learn to live with our losses in a way that allows us to love again. I saw myself as I helped Patrick write this book. You may see yourself as well.

Sylvester Monroe
November 29, 2010

"He Restoreth My Soul ..."
– David
Psalms 23.4

Part One

CHAPTER I

Take My Breath Away

Love is there, no matter what dreams may come...

Dreams often serve our destiny. They in some ways foretell our fortune and in some cases retell our histories. No one ever taught me how to dream. Dreams are as natural to me as the breath I take. My challenge has been to distinguish fears that seep into my subconscious against divine impressions of what my life and love should be.

I was five years old the first time I lost a woman that I loved. My maternal grandmother Lois, a petite, light-skinned woman with long beautiful brunette hair, lived in Chicago's South Side Chatham neighborhood not far from my mother and me. She was a seductive socialite passionately in love with life and her family and friends. And I was in love with her as only a kindergartener could be. I called her "Gran."

Gran spent her off-time as a church musician and Sunday school teacher who thought she could fix anything and solve any problem. I loved watching her on Saturday nights when she'd read lessons from the Sunday school book with Billie Holiday playing on the record player and a glass of wine on the table beside her.

In my young eyes, there was absolutely nothing she couldn't do. One day while she was working in the garden behind her house, I heard her yell my name.

"Patrick! Patrick! Help me! Help me!" she cried.

I ran out into the yard to see her slowly sinking into a wet hole that sucked her down deeper and deeper like quicksand. I ran to her. I couldn't speak. I just acted. With my thin, short arms, I reached to pull her out, but I wasn't strong enough and couldn't hold on to her. As she slipped through my hands, I sat by the hole and cried.

I kept hearing her last words to me: "Help me, Patrick! Help me!"

Terribly shaken, I suddenly felt myself move on the couch where I was sleeping. I woke up with tears in my eyes and a tremendous sense of loss, accompanied by overwhelming panic and fear. With my heart still racing and my face flushed and wet with tears, I jumped up, ran to the telephone and called her. When I heard her voice, a calming wave swept over me, as I realized it was all a horrible dream. I never told her about it. I didn't want her to worry, and was embarrassed by feelings that I couldn't totally understand at the time.

I don't think I ever looked at my grandmother the same way again. In fact, from that night on, whenever I saw her I always feared that somehow, someday she'd leave me. I feared one day I'd call and she wouldn't be there, and that no matter how hard I tried, I ultimately wouldn't have the strength to hold on to her and keep her from leaving me again.

The dream about my grandmother was not the last time I had a boyhood nightmare about being separated from a woman I loved. In another dream, when I was about seven years old, I was in a big house with windows that opened onto a great field where I could hear my friends playing. But instead of going out to play with my friends, I wanted to be in the house with my mother, who for me is the definition of beauty. Like my grandmother, she was petite with distinctive Native American features: deep-set eyes, high cheekbones and long, silky, wavy hair. She was funny and a wonderful cook. I knocked and knocked and called out to her, but she was on the other side of a big door. Though I continued to knock, she wouldn't answer. I knew she was in there, and I knew she heard me. I could hear her heart beating on the other side of the door. But she would not open it. No matter how hard I knocked, called out to her and cried, she would not let me in. So I sat outside the door, leaned my face on it to be closer to her and cried till I lay asleep at the foot of the door. I refused to leave until she came out, but she never did.

Sigmund Freud would have had a field day with these dreams, or maybe he'd find them terribly simplistic. But they've never left me, and what I know now is that in the past they colored my adult relationships, including my marriage, with every woman I've ever loved. For most of my life, it seems I've tried in vain to hold on to them or to get them to let me in and be part of their lives, but to no avail.

I'm thirty-five years old, the pastor of a growing, urban congregation and, like millions of Americans — divorced. The calling to the pastorate certainly did not save me from the painful sense of loss that accompanies divorce or rescue me from the paralyzing fear of starting my life over again. After Sunday's service is over and I walk into my home I'm alone again, still a guy subject to the gamut of human emotions that come with such a traumatic experience. I'm on my own now and have been for some time. There are upsides to aloneness: peace, quiet, and tranquility, time for reflection, to take inventory of my needs, and rediscover who I am. In fact, being alone has become my default experience of life since I was a child. For in my solitude, I've found the most precious gift God has given any of us and that is— me.

Luther

I miss Luther.

Luther Vandross sang about love and longing in ways that only the Divine really understands. His voice was confusing to the soul, resonating in ways that made us simultaneously hopeful and sad and always longing for more. When I first heard "A House is Not a Home" I was a young man, sixteen or seventeen perhaps. I felt his passion and was moved by his words, but I didn't fully understand the powerful meaning of those lyrics. *"A chair is still a chair even when there's no one sitting there. But a house is not a home when there's no one there..."* When I think about how much I paid for my furniture, if I could get a refund, I would. Life has taught me that material things are not the best filler for an empty human heart.

I've observed love in many contexts, and at some point I figured out that every love story doesn't have a happy ending and that sometimes the old saying, "It's better to have loved and lost than never to have loved at all" is more than mere words. It was difficult to admit that and yet sobering to understand that all love may not last a lifetime and that just because we sometimes don't get to keep the love we wanted doesn't mean it was not love at all. I think it's harmful and unhealthy to devalue relationships just because they didn't meet our expectations.

As far back as I can remember I've had big-family dreams: kids running around the house, a barbeque pit out back, a warm and welcoming home made with a loving companion. But all that's faded now with the passage of time. I've come to a place in life where I no longer demand that it give me everything I want. Whether I marry again remains an open question, but faith is a powerful thing. Faith moves us to perpetually ask the most important questions until our blinded eyes are opened and we see the answer before us. Through my faith I was able to resurrect and reconstruct love within my subjective consciousness. That same faith still provokes me to ask questions and challenges me to love again.

Love, like football, is full contact. I pastor a congregation, and I suppose it would be easier just to get married again for the sake of having an acceptable social relationship and for the advancement of my career. People in my vocation do it all the time, but marriage does not always presuppose love, and love must be actualized to truly fulfill the heart.

Breakups, separations, and divorce are like emotional tsunamis. They change the human spirit forever and alter us in ways that take a diligent heart, a keen, loving eye, and a steady hand to love again. The good news is that storms end and dark nights don't last forever. There's recovery after the storm, but it leaves us uncertain about the future. Sometimes the water washes away things we can never regain. It can destroy what we thought we could never live without. For a while, I didn't know if I'd ever recover, and admittedly I didn't know if I really wanted to. Sometimes we get comfortable in the floodwaters. My pain was nourishing and my depression was like a pillow that I learned to rest and rely on.

Regaining a healthy perspective isn't easy. Even as I write this, I'm still being transformed by my faith and every day I rediscover what I need to take the next step in my journey.

Without a hint of bravado, this book is priceless for me because writing it has clarified my understanding, and that has been so expensive for me. I had to live it and did not have the luxury of doing so privately.

In the coming pages, I'll be open and honest about my story. I wrestled with how candid to be and came to the conclusion that to be anything less than completely honest would be a fruitless exercise in vanity. So I determined to be brave. My Gran says I have a lot of nerve, and as always, she's right. But, in this case, my nerviness and bravery may help others by expressing some valuable observations of love and loss. Indeed, as much as you may need to hear my story (and I hope you do), I have a greater need to tell it.

Breakups, broken heartedness, and divorce don't discriminate. Regardless of race, age, gender, sexual orientation, or religious upbringing, they can and do leave anyone in its wake affected by the aftermath. Surely there are worse things in life that can happen to a person, and I knew it wasn't the end of the world for me, but it sure felt like it at the time. I made it though, and you can too.

I won't waste time debating the "rightness" or "wrongness" of divorce. There's plenty of writing in that area. I won't expand upon archaic and benign ideologies that permeate religious conservatism and mainstream Western culture. These words are meant to describe the reality of living through divorce and loss, and regaining one's faith rather than a theoretical view of it.

"We don't believe in divorce, so we don't carry any books on the subject," a clerk said to me after I searched a Christian bookstore for something to read shortly after my divorce. Hurting badly, I was seeking medicine for my soul. I was stunned and taken aback. The Christian church to which I'd pledged my life was telling me that it had nothing at all to say to me on this subject. I eventually found voices with much to say, but their words were empty.

As a sacred caregiver, I believe the Creator is very much acquainted with our realities. When I see over half the marriages in this country end in divorce, I believe that as a church we should have more to say than simply, it is a sin. The issues of marital dissolution are more complex than the thoughtless, often insensitive platitudes that course through sermons all around the country from Sunday to Sunday. We must push the discourse forward to a safe, non-punitive place where we're allowed to construct useful conversations about divorce rather than cover it up. My mother says, "Things that are covered don't heal well," and I agree with her.

This book is meant to be a provocative work that challenges us to think and re-think the wonderful and fluid idea of loving again. To love again is a discipline of the soul and spirit. But before I could ponder loving someone else again, I had to do what I'd never done — learn to love myself.

"As an African American man, don't you feel obligated to find an African American woman, get married, have a family and pass on your genes?" a female friend once asked. "You seem pretty smart and you clean up okay. Don't you feel an obligation to your race?"

Pressure came from everywhere; people all around me were concernd with when I was going to marry again and who I was going to love next. Her questions resonated with me because of what they said about a black woman's view of an African American male's sexuality. In the most simplistic way, they were affirming. Double standards about interracial dating remain quite common. I'm well aware as an African American man that if I date outside my race it raises questions about my love for my own people. If an African American woman dates outside her race, it may be viewed as a justifiable necessity because of a perceived shortage of eligible black men.

Mr. Shaffer

My grandfather has been gone for about thirteen years now. One of 14 children who migrated north from West Point, Mississippi to Chicago, he was a World War II veteran who did not except the GI

Bill benefits offered by the government. Instead, he went to work for a utility company after the war.

Shaffer is a German-Irish name given to my great-grandfather by the plantation owner our family worked for. My grandfather was a tall, thin man with well-defined Cherokee features. He was always finely dressed and frequented Chicago's jazz clubs, where he never missed Count Basie, John Coltrane, and Billie Holiday whenever they came to town during the 1940s, 50s, and 60s.

By the time I was seven or eight, I was aware of who he was, but his once thick, black hair was all but gone. The fine salt and pepper wisps that were left were beautiful to the eye. He retired some two decades after his divorce from my grandmother and after that his life pretty much consisted of work in his backyard garden, the Chicago Cubs, Budweiser beer, and brown liquor.

One day about three years ago, I saw a billboard advertisement for Seagram's Crown Royal whiskey. I'd never paid attention to it before, but that day I noticed something familiar in the ad — it was the gold-trimmed, purple Crown Royal bag. At first, I couldn't recall why the bag was so familiar. I sat stumped at the traffic light until honking horns jarred me, forcing me to drive on.

Finally, I remembered. As children, my oldest brother and I would visit Grandfather's house. One of our chores was to take bags of coins he saved for us to the bank. We were always excited to see how much each of us would get for the coins. I'd always thought the bags came from the bank and that all banks supplied such bags for customers. Seeing the Crown Royal bag in the billboard ad made me realize that my grandfather may have drunk the liquor that came in those bags. I was devastated.

Then I remembered a trip to Mississippi on the Greyhound. Grandfather packed food for our midnight departure from Union Station. We had juice boxes. Grandfather had a pitcher of brown liquid.

"Grandfather, what's in the pitcher?" I asked.

"Its tea, Pat," he replied.

"I like tea. Can I have some?"

"No, you have juice."

He never gave me any of what was in that pitcher. But I do remember him sharing whatever it was with a stranger on the bus. They passed white Styrofoam cups all night.

As he got older, he developed Alzheimer's, a disease that separates the body from the mind. Those who have it slowly recede into what doctors call a second childhood. Our family took him in when he could no longer take care of himself. We did our best but just couldn't give him all he needed at home. So we put him into a nursing facility where he could receive 24-hour care.

Eventually, this handsome, vibrant man became a shell of what he once was. I remember coming home from college to see him without telling anyone. I went alone. The disease had progressed to the point that he had to be restrained, and I walked into a dim room where he was strapped to a chair facing the window. He wasn't fighting to get loose. He was merely there. His eyes were drooped and sunken, and his chin rested on his chest. I wasn't prepared for what I saw and how it made me feel.

I'd never seen him unable to recognize me. There had never been a time when I looked into his eyes and he did not flash that wonderful, toothless grin back at me. But this time I walked in, sat down before him, and looked into his eyes. There was nothing there. Fighting back tears, I pondered his fate and wondered if it would someday be mine. I pulled my chair closer to his and touched his bony knee, trying to make some connection with him. But the man I knew was gone. My sorrow turned to anger as I looked at him and a tremendous wave of hopelessness swept over me.

Could this happen to me? When would it come? The questions swirled in my head as I grew more frustrated and angry. I slid my chair closer to him, stood up slightly, and whispered in his ear.

"It won't happen to me like it happened to you," I said. As I sat back down, he stopped rocking and for just a moment glared up at me. A cold chill ran down my arm as he turned away and began to rock back and forth in his chair again.

One day there'll be nothing left for me to do but die. But I made up my mind then and there that, until death's calls; I would live and love as long as I can. My decision was not a judgment of him. It was a piece of wisdom from a dying old man given to me as his mind and body withered away. After war, marriage, divorce, and retirement, at some point my grandfather no longer had anything to love that would love him back. There were many things he loved in his life, but the objects of his affection could not love him back. Watching him die riddled with cancer and starving for love, I learned that we must live till there is no life left and we must love until our hearts are empty. At that point the only thing death can take away from us is our breath.

CHAPTER II

Faded Pictures

There are no images left of us, nothing tangible to prove we ever were. Just still pictures in my mind, stunning but faded by time.

I still remember the hot, summer Sunday night I met Denae. I was visiting the church in the western suburbs of Chicago where I grew up when I saw her. Denae didn't see me, and what struck me first about her is what initially attracts all men to a woman. She was absolutely beautiful. I remember everything about her that night. Her quintessential 90s chic style on her petite, five-foot-five-inch frame, the gold, herringboned necklace with a name plate that spelled out her name, and the hazel skin, brown eyes, high cheekbones, and skinny legs. She rivaled my mother and sisters, who I thought were the most beautiful women I'd ever seen until that night. She was beautiful in ways I had not even imagined.

Funny thing is I almost left without speaking to her that night. I was about to get into my car when I decided to turn back and find her. I couldn't tell you exactly why, but I knew that I wanted to hear her voice and look into her eyes. As I was walking up the steps she was coming down them. I remember those big doe eyes and that half smile as I reached out to introduce myself and shake hands. I remember the gentle touch of her hand in mine. I remember the deep, soft tone of her voice. First impressions are powerful, and sometimes it's the small things that really snare a man's heart.

Denae, however, did not seem nearly as impressed with me. I was an eighteen-year-old, budding evangelist and aspiring pastor who'd been working in ministry all my life, I was just embracing a more specific calling to lead. My eyes were wide to the possibility and promise of greatness that resonated in my heart. I had grand dreams of writing, teaching, traveling, and winning souls to Christ, as we would say then. From the time I was very young, my plans were big.

Early in life, I also developed a way with women, usually meeting them in class or through a mutual friend, never really having to extend myself much to make someone's acquaintance. That was great for a terribly introverted guy like me. This time, though, I could not believe that this woman who I just had to know did not seem as pleased to know *me*! I was in no way used to such a reaction from the opposite sex.

Undaunted, I came back week after week to my childhood church until we exchanged telephone numbers. We started off having long "getting to know you" conversations. Though we talked and talked and talked, much of that short summer has become a blur for me, not because it was insignificant, but because the time passed so quickly even as it stood still in the moments we shared. I can't remember one conversation we had, but I remember how every minute on the phone with her made me feel that she and I were the only two people in the world.

That fall she was leaving to go to school in Florida and I was heading for school in Oklahoma. We stayed in touch the best we could for two young people whose lives were rapidly racing forward. A year or two later, we found ourselves back in Chicago and seeing each other more frequently. The following summer was when we first kissed. We would sit on her parents' front porch talking for hours, and one night under a full moon, it happened. I wish I could remember what we talked about. Truthfully, at that moment, I honestly didn't care. Her presence was intoxicating, her voice spellbinding, like good music. There's so much to be said about being with someone you love. We're never more conscious of living than when we're connected to someone. Life can be full and whole as a single person — yet having someone to share it with makes you aware that those moments are a grace from God. The night we first kissed, I was about to leave her on the porch, we embraced and as natural as it is to breathe our lips met. At that moment, I knew I wanted her close to me forever.

That was only the beginning. On the books, we were married five years. In reality, we lived together less than two years and were separated for three. As I write this, if we'd stayed together, we would have been married fourteen years. It seems a lifetime ago.

During the eight years we've been divorced, there have been some rough times for both of us trying to cope with loss, guilt, anger, and acceptance. We've had conversations about what went wrong, of things not said, and words spoken the wrong way. We've apologized to each other and wished each other the best.

Today, Denae is more beautiful than the day we married. She is an accomplished educator. We're both doing what we talked about doing some fifteen years ago. We're just doing it without each other.

Since my divorce there's been only one woman that I seriously considered marrying. But for better or worse, it didn't happen. So my former wife is to this point the only one to get me down the aisle to say, "I do." Having her in my life changed me in ways that I could not have imagined. She made me a better person when she came into my life, and she did the same when she left.

When we were married, what hampered my growth in love was that I thought love presupposed pleasure. So if love did not make me feel good then I did not think it was love at all. As I've grown, my understanding of love has been broadened by a host of experiences. I understand now that love has a duplicitous nature. It brings both pleasure and pain. I know now that we'll never have any more love than we make. Making love in this sense means recognizing the virtue and redemption in all the ingredients that the soul has gathered, and being wise enough to love the being that brought all these scattered pieces together.

I have not found a way to "un-love" my ex-wife. I've tried. But that's as impossible as it is to un-sleep with someone. It can't be done. I loved her then and I love her now. I don't want to mislead you. There were times when I hated her, when I cursed the day I met her. Then I hated myself because underneath my anger was pain and love. Divorce and break-ups are just our human way of dramatically and legally redefining relationships.

I've had some dark moments, hungering for relief from the pain that at times seemed too much to bear. I still have them, just not as frequently as before. I didn't know when the pain would end or if it ever would. When the divorce was final, to my surprise, it still wasn't over. I ached from loneliness and missed her terribly. My depression was deep, and complicated by the fact that I was working in church leadership and not able to grieve privately. My pain was fodder for speculation, innuendo, and the like. When my divorce was final, no one looked me in the face and asked how I was doing or asked me what I was feeling. It made me sad to know that our witness of Christian love fails us when issues hit too close for comfort. I was alone again, and my pain was aggravated by the aloneness that I loved and loathed. I didn't think I was going to recover.

Part of my job at the church was to go to the hospital when we learned that a member had passed away or was near death. One instance stands out. When I got a call that a church member was dying, I rushed to the hospital and found her surprisingly lucid and coherent.

"I thought you were dying," I said with a smile.

"I am," she said. "There's nothing they can do, and I signed a DNR."

"What's a DNR?" I asked.

"It means Do Not Resuscitate," she replied. "If I stop breathing, I don't want them to resuscitate me. I am ready to die," she said plainly.

I prayed with her, kissed her on the cheek, and then said goodbye. The call came the next day that she had indeed passed away. I pondered what it meant not to want to live and I also pondered not wanting to love again. Maybe after break-ups and divorce we have a DNR for our souls. We don't want our feelings to be resuscitated because loving is just way too hard. My own depression was palpable — I'd come home, sit on the floor, and cry. But my tears did not always flow. It was more a sorrow of the soul. I was hurting but couldn't explain why. I didn't know how to pinpoint my pain. Even if I did, I knew I couldn't begin to translate my feelings into words.

CHAPTER III

Lemonade

Somewhere between sweetness and bitterness is where the heart lives in love, but hearts aren't meant to live alone.

I've been making lemonade for as long as I can remember. My grandmother told me I make the best lemonade in the world. Give me some fresh lemons and a few other ingredients that I won't divulge, and I can make lemonade that would make you shout for joy.

Making a good life, like making good lemonade, depends on the mix of ingredients. When it comes to lemonade, my secret is the delicate balance between sweet and sour. It's one of my spiritual gifts. I've been using it all my life, not just to make lemonade, but to weigh the balance of experiences that have brought joy and sorrow into my life.

Since childhood, I've understood that if you can blend all the elements and strike the right balance, life, like lemonade, can be tasty and refreshing. I believe the same is true of love.

As a young man in my early twenties, I cherished the sweetness of love, basking in the pleasure of my young wife's warm, effervescent femininity. Her tender love and care sustained my growing masculine heart and nourished my soul.

What I could not except easily and would not embrace fully was another side of my wife that quite frankly made me crazy and drove a wedge between us. In reflection, her needling and our confrontations were typical of young couples whose lives come together and then pull apart as their histories collide.

At those times, it was difficult to even talk with each other. I'd sit and listen without being emotionally present; often feeling more like a student being lectured to by a persistent teacher than an adult capable of thinking for himself. I became a master of being there but not being there, silently tucking away my heart when I feared it would be hurt. I learned how to be dutiful but without any compassion in the doing.

I look over my shoulder at that young man and have great pity for him because he didn't know that love is an all encompassing affair, with bitter and sweet times that can bring a happy life when stirred together into a healthy mix. I developed love fantasies very early on watching Disney classics like *Cinderella*, and pictured my lovely princess who'd be mine happily ever after — just like in the movies. While those ideas were sweet and sincere and very real, they were also an incomplete and unrealistic foundation upon which to build and sustain lifelong, life-giving relationships. I couldn't understand at the time that love is not always sweet, and that if it is only sweet, it can't yield the necessary ingredients for a full and satisfying life.

Winter's Dream

We got married on a beautiful Saturday morning, unusually warm for that time of year. The wedding was somewhat anticlimactic for me. I kept thinking, *we planned this for over a year, spent all this money, and it's over in 19 minutes.* I always thought it would be more. I wasn't sure how, but it seemed to be lacking in some way. I'm a guy, and I've never been in love with weddings. In fact, I found the whole process a bit patronizing. Essentially, the wedding is not about us; it's about the bride. We're mere props, or at best bit players, in an extravagant stage play. We're told where to stand, what to wear, when to speak, and when to leave. The wedding to me was an overdramatized formality leading to what I really wanted, a beautiful life with the woman I adored. So I breathed deeply and indulged. It was sweet labor.

I would give her the day she wanted, and I'd have the night I wanted. I decided that was pretty good as long as I didn't have to do the wedding thing again anytime soon. We began within fifteen minutes of the scheduled start time, and the ceremony ended without any mishaps. But there was one thing about that day that sometimes still haunts me.

As the pastor blessed the rings, my best man handed him my wife's ring. I was proud of that ring. I'd worked a third shift job to get her something nice. It was a one-carat, marquise-cut diamond surrounded in baguettes, which added a second carat. I haven't seen the ring in years and never asked for it back. But I've wondered about it. The ring embodied the promise of a loving future. To me it was a down payment on our lifelong love.

When a man loves a woman, he'll work hard for her. As long as she's grateful, a man will give all he has. It was all I had at that moment, a ring and a promise that she'd always love me. As the pastor blessed her ring, I felt proud and scared. I wanted to do my best. I wanted to make love proud. When it was time for me to place the ring on her finger, the pastor handed it to me. The ring was in two parts, the main ring and its attachment.

As I reached for the ring, I dropped it. I still don't know what happened. I was startled. Everyone was looking at me — I'd dropped the ring. I certainly didn't mean to. I don't know if I was distracted, careless, or just nervous, but I knelt down, picked up the ring, then turned and held it up so everyone could see. We all laughed and moved on. But I've never forgotten that I dropped the ring that day. Part of me has still not forgiven myself. I've often thought in the years since that my issue isn't finding love — it's holding onto it. It always seems to slip away just when I want most to take it and make it mine. It falls between my fingers like sand, or a diamond ring that slipped from my fingers on my wedding day.

From my theological upbringing, I've always understood God in antiquity to be the One God in three persons, or expressions. I have many friends who ascribe to a Oneness theology, with which I don't entirely disagree. But as I've listened, read, and meditated for over twenty-five years now, I've come to a profound understanding that God is complicated, or at least multi-layered. So like God, so like us all. We are all layered in various ways, and life brings out different facets of our oneness in different seasons and for different reasons. I pastor a church, but I am also a son, brother, friend, sacred-activist, playwright, actor, and singer. Yet all these layers make up just one person — me. Mothers and fathers, for example, are more than just caregivers and providers. They are multi-layered people who require love and recognition on every level.

One thing that contributed to the demise of my marriage was the incompleteness of our individual selves. We were twenty-two, brimming with energy and optimism about life, but we quickly learned that love and marriage are not by default as self satisfying as we were led to believe. We were so young and so unfinished in many ways.

Love and marriage have a particular set of needs that constantly demand time and attention. But people in a marriage also have individual needs that cannot be ignored. Relationships without such consideration and nurturing will ultimately fail. As I've gotten older and seen friends, careers, and life goals change, I've discovered that things don't simply work out by themselves. In every area of life, intentionality is key for success.

The Married Life

Life happened fast after our wedding. We were not prepared. We loved each other, but didn't fully trust each other yet. Every small thing escalated into a big issue.

Our first trip to the grocery store exploded into a three-hour adventure in futility. She wanted to make a list. I never made a list, but she relentlessly insisted on explaining why a list was important. The "Grocery List Lecture" was the first of many that I endured the first year and a half of our marriage. In hindsight she may have been right about the value of a grocery list. But at twenty-two, I had no interest in listening to someone who sounded a lot like my mother.

At the grocery store, we also discovered there were very few things we both liked. She liked Breyer's, I liked Häagen-Dazs. She liked margarine, I liked butter. And neither of us wanted to compromise. That resulted in silly, but very real "turf wars." So I got my own shopping cart and filled it with the things I liked. I felt liberated. An hour later, we met at the checkout line. She had a full basket, I had a full basket, and neither of us had conceded.

I guess we felt it would be giving away too much power when we're just getting to know each other. So there was a standoff as we surveyed each other's grocery baskets. At some point after another hour of discourse on dishwashing detergent and toothpaste, we decided the whole thing was pretty silly. Unfortunately, we'd fail to find middle ground on even bigger and more important issues. Many times the differences led to acrimony. But that night in the grocery store we worked it out. If only we could've lived there forever. One afternoon my wife called me at work, and it wasn't the usual greeting.

"I'm late," she snapped.

"For what?"

"Stop playing. My period hasn't come, and it's your fault!"

"Okay. Let's talk this evening after work."

I hung up the phone and walked outside to get some air. My emotions and thoughts were in turmoil. For sure, I wanted a house full of children, and I wanted them with my wife. But things weren't good between us, and I was more concerned about our relationship than starting a family. We'd been married less than nine months, and our future was uncertain. We often said mean things to each other, or would just shut down completely and say nothing at all.

As a young husband, I thought my job was to make my wife happy, and I wanted her to be happy. But right from the beginning of our marriage I felt I was failing all the time. Feminine emotions have always perplexed me, and I was growing more confused every day. I felt if she was having a bad day, then somehow it was my fault. If she didn't like her life, I was supposed to fix it. Her happiness was my responsibility, and I took being a husband seriously even when I seemed unable to help her.

I prayed a lot in those days, for her and myself. I wanted us to work. But it wasn't working, and now she might be pregnant. I knew she didn't want to have children then and neither did I. There were so many things she hadn't yet accomplished, and we were still having a running conversation about juggling life pursuits and managing a family one day.

Going home that night, a lump stuck in my throat and nausea filled my stomach. I didn't know what to expect. If your wife says, "Honey I might be pregnant," your emotional and verbal response must be supportive and go something like: "Honey, the last time we made love I prayed quietly that this would be the night you would conceive our love child and when I woke up this morning I prayed to God Almighty that you would tell me this news today. I am so happy ..."

I was young then, so when I walked through the door, my biggest fear was that I was going to be blamed. But the issue for me was much deeper than the pregnancy itself. My concern was what a pregnancy meant for us.

It was a warm fall day, and the sun was setting as I came home. We opened the window and sat on the floor facing one another. And that evening we talked well into the night. I've always been an optimist with the ability to wrestle down my own cynicism. I was young and strong. My dreams and hopes were alive, and I believed that no matter what happened we'd be okay. As long as I could look in her eyes and know in my heart that we were together, I felt there wasn't anything that we wouldn't conquer. She was all I needed. The very thought of her was my weapon against discouragement.

"We're going to be okay," I told her. It was late and we'd talked ourselves into a few hopeful scenarios that allowed a ray of happiness to sneak upon us. "We might be having a baby!"

In the glow of that happy moment, we decided to find out right then and headed to Walgreens to buy a pregnancy test. I was amazed and annoyed at how expensive they were.

"If it costs this much, can we wash it off and use it again later?"

She shook her head, rolled her eyes, and we bought the test. As soon as we got home, she took the test. It was the longest eight minutes of my life. We decided to leave the stick in the bathroom and wait outside together with a timer. We tried to make small talk and we took turns wrestling each other down when one of us wanted to see the stick before it was time. We even laughed some that night. We entered the bathroom at the same time, and the timer went off. The test stick had a minus sign on it. We were not pregnant. We hugged and let out a collective sigh of relief. Then we looked into each other's eyes for a moment and shared an unspoken sadness that passed between us before going to bed.

That night I couldn't sleep. In some ways, I felt closer to her. Years later after we divorced people would say, "I bet you're glad you didn't have any children." At first I'd answer, "Yes." But over the years that response has changed. As I've matured and longed for family and watched my friends start families (those children are now 10, 11, 12 years old now), I wonder what the face of our child might have looked like by now. My house is empty and there are no signs that we were ever married.

After that night, I started thinking more earnestly about supporting a family and preparing for the day when we'd have children. I wanted a better job, and I found one working at a prestigious investment firm. I had a safety net that would cushion another unexpected pregnancy scare, and I was happy. I didn't particularly like my boss, a middle-aged Irish woman with short hair. We didn't connect, and I did not try to be warm with her. We disagreed about some procedure that I thought wasn't in the best interest of our customers and I voiced my concern.

The job had me flying between Chicago and Boston every week for at least three days a week. It didn't sit well with my new wife. I didn't think I'd be away so much, but I had to work so I chose not to complain. I was doing this for our future. She grumbled but there was not a whole lot that could be done.

After a ninety-day probationary period, I was called into the department head's office and was informed that after evaluating my performance and acclimation to their culture, they did not find my engagement satisfactory and were letting me go. I was stunned! I walked into that office like the proverbial deer caught in headlights. Someone walked me back to my desk to gather all my things. I then went to the HR department and the director was very sympathetic. All I could say, as if quietly thinking out loud, was "I just got married."

I gathered my belongings and headed to the car. My wife and I had a routine of driving to work together. I'd drop her off in the mornings, go to my job, and then pick her up after work and head home. I had all of seven minutes to figure out how I felt about what had just happened and an honest way to tell my wife that I was unemployed. My head was spinning. I felt like I had to vomit, and I was sweating. I was in shock.

I'd never been fired before, and they didn't prepare me for this in premarital counseling. I don't know how I drove to her that day. Our marriage was bad and life didn't seem like it was working. And I was growing wearier every day. She got in the car and said hello, but I couldn't talk. I can't remember if I was breathing or not. I couldn't look at her. I was staring straight ahead, motionless. She asked what was wrong, but I still couldn't speak. My throat was locked. I'm not sure how I was still driving.

Finally, I cleared my throat. But whatever I was about to say never made it out. I just burst into tears. All I could say was, "I'm sorry." She didn't know what was going on and by this time she was in a full panic. We pulled over to the side of the street and I buried my face in a wad of tissue and began to tell her what happened. I still couldn't look at her. I was ashamed. I promised her parents that I'd take care of their daughter and now I'd brought our marriage to a dangerous precipice we might never recover from.

She asked questions, and I gave all the answers I had. I was still processing it myself. I couldn't wait for the sun to go down that night; I wanted to hide from the world. What ached so badly was that I loved her and didn't mind working for her. When a man loves a woman he'll work for her and try his best to provide for her and her children. I'd worked since I was a teenager. For the first time in my life, I was unemployed. I was so scared. For a moment, I blamed her. I reasoned that if I hadn't been married I'd still be working, or if I'd taken the other job offer that I'd gotten, I'd still be working. So somehow this was her fault. I even blamed God.

"God, how could you do this to me? I'm trying the best I can, and the more I try the worse things get." I was depressed and felt alienated from her. She was not supportive. I remember her saying, "My daddy always worked. I didn't get married to be the only one working. I can go back home."

Her words stung, but my first inclination was not to dwell on how her words made me feel but to reassure her that things would be okay. I held those words against her for years until I began to understand how scared she was too. She sounded harsh and uncaring, but at that moment those scolding words were all she had to give. Still, I needed her support. When a man doesn't have a job he feels less than a man. There is no remedy for that other than feeling like you're providing for your loved ones. At twenty-two, I defined myself by the numbers on my paycheck and my self-esteem rose and fell with her opinion of me. I thought my life was over at twenty-two and that I'd never recover. But as I learned not to rely on her opinion of me to define who I was, I began to learn things about myself that would serve me for years to come. Most importantly, I learned that strength is found in low moments, and with God's help I began to discover who I was even as my marriage grew sicker and never recovered.

Love Storm

It is said that love is a many-splendored thing. I've discovered that for the full richness of love to flourish, it must encompass both pain and pleasure. In a *Vibe* magazine article about Rick James right after he passed, a passage from his eulogy said:

Don't you know pain is the mother of creativity? Did you know without pain in your life, you wouldn't be able to appreciate pleasure? Without hell in your life, you would never understand heaven? Rick's life was full of pain and struggle. But through that pain and that struggle shined a star of genius.

It is pain that often justifies our love and spawns the connections needed to enjoy all the pleasure love has to offer.

I don't look at my former marriage as a failure. Over time as we walk further and further away from some moments, we begin to have a different perspective on things. We cannot measure the damage of a tornado until it's passed. Once it's over, we're able to assess the potency of the storm, what's been taken and what remains. Sometimes the most amazing thing about storms is not the damage they do, but what's left unharmed by fierce winds and ferocious waves. Precious things can be spared despite terrible wind, rain, and lightning. But we never know until it passes, and we mine the wreckage to discover what the storm didn't destroy.

I can't say my marriage was stormier, with all its challenges and unexpected twists and turns, than any other new marriage. However stormy it was, I have learned that storms don't stay forever. And they have a way of washing away things we'll never find again while simultaneously uncovering good things that were hidden from view.

After the storm is when you begin to evaluate what's most precious and what can be let go. It's there that we learn about the things in our lives that the storm will never be strong enough to take away from us.

What Must Be

I've resolved that in life some things must be, and the best course is simply to "let it happen." I've fought sometimes to stop things from happening, fighting for control when I had no control. I've learned that events occur in our lives that God designs to happen. And I've learned to accept pain and circumstances I'd rather not experience as a natural part of life. Job asked, "Shall we receive good at the hand of God, and not receive evil?" Job understood that life, in a sense, is a book and we're not the authors. While that can be troubling, there's also great peace in knowing it.

Prior to the divorce becoming final, I was alone for a couple of years. At first it was peaceful, no more arguments and no more trying to make someone happy, knowing that somehow I was going to fail. I desperately wanted to be free but just didn't know how. Separation and divorce involve two distinct lifestyles that carry two distinct sets of emotions. When I was separated, I felt like my life was between floors. Like an animal cruelly tied to a pole, I could move only so far and only for so long, and I was okay with that. Then it became frustrating because I needed to be done with this moment in my life so I could start thinking about rebuilding.

On the day my divorce was finalized, I remember walking away from the courtroom feeling winded and a bit dizzy. Women tend to think that men don't feel when a relationship breaks up, but I was hurting terribly. My heart was crushed as I sat in the courtroom waiting for the judge to call the case. I was listening to the other proceedings and thinking to myself, *how did I get here? What happened and when did it happen? Is this really happening?*

Sometimes, divorce, like death, can be merciful. I remember going to the theater to see Mel Gibson's *The Passion of the Christ*. As I watched Jesus beaten over and over, and saw him suffer, I began to meditate on the utility of death in the human experience. I began to understand that death can be compassionate in bringing great suffering to an end. Divorce also can be a responsible, kind, and just decision when the people in a marriage have been so damaged that continuing is neither wise nor responsible. The prevailing view of divorce — it's wrong and one of the most egregious of sins — comes mostly from people who've never experienced it personally. Yet, I've also heard many a preacher change his rhetoric after experiencing divorce first hand.

When it was legally over, peace and sadness ran simultaneously through my mind. I'd lived on my own for three years, but coming home that night seemed so much harder than it ever had before. I walked through the door, as I had countless times before, with no one there. But that night it felt emptier than it ever had before. That night, when I laid in bed on "my side" and then rolled over, the reality hit me that she was gone and I cried myself to sleep, night after night after night. For months I couldn't bring myself to sleep in the middle of the bed. From that moment on I noticed the emptiness more than ever before. Riding alone in the car or sitting in a movie theater with no one next to me were not-so-subtle reminders of the loss.

In the Gospel of St. John, it amazes me how self-possessed and aware Jesus was in a moment of great stress. Praying to God, He seems to be reporting that all his disciples were with him and are accounted for except this "one." Everybody is here Lord, Jesus says, except Judas. We can have everything but we are most sensitive to what is not there, and having everything except that one missing thing can drive us into spaces and places in our own emotions that are significantly hard to come out of.

My life is full right now, and I shouldn't complain. I'm grateful for my work, my family, and friends old and new. I'm relatively happy, and feel fulfilled yet classically impatient with the slowness of my forwardness in personal endeavors. I shouldn't complain because I have more than many others, and God has blessed me. But I still can't help notice what's missing. I can smile and laugh and go about life as usual, but when I wake up in the morning I see that I don't have what I once had — maybe what I never had, and if honest, it bothers me. So like Jesus, I pray and say: "Hey, God, I have all the wonderful gifts you gave me, except that one thing that's missing. Can you help me out with this?"

That's when I think about making lemonade. When we discover what we truly want, we begin to see all the bittersweet lemons life has to offer and the wonderful life we can make from them.

CHAPTER IV

Dark Victory

Love is never frightened by the absence of light, love shines as brightly in the dark as it does in daylight. As day fades into night, love lights our longings and amplifies frail voices. When we can't find love, love finds us.

"How do you feel about that?" the therapist asked.

"I don't know. Your question makes me uncomfortable. Nobody ever asked me that before."

Ask most people how long they were married, and it's a simple question that prompts a simple response. But when people ask me that, there are always two answers. One number is the length of time we were legally married. The other is the time we actually lived in the same house together.

After the separation, I moved into my own apartment. At 27 years old, it was the first time I'd ever lived on my own. Emotional adrenaline was high. But I was not yet conscious of my own deep hurt. I had not begun the journey of self-discovery that would eventually free me not just from marriage but also from a deep childhood bruising I didn't even know I was carrying. Quite frankly, I wouldn't let myself embrace the truth of what was happening to me then. Nothing in my culture or religion gave me the tools to be honest with God or myself to be the person I needed to be for a healthy mental and spiritual life. Instead, what both culture and religion offered me was just the opposite — ways to avoid the truth and emotional baggage, to hate myself for things that were my fault and some that were not.

It was two years before we officially divorced. When we first separated, I was okay with that. She was gone, and I was glad. I was alone, but there was peace and quiet. Suddenly, I had to do things for myself that I'd relied on her to do. I had to learn the domestic chores that often escape a man's view when he lives with a woman. I look back and realize I didn't know just how dependent I was on her. I had only viewed my life, my love, and God as being attached to my relationship with her. Without her, I was learning how to stand on my own. I began to understand that I didn't need the blanket of her warm security to cover me. I was learning how to knit my own.

I loved my apartment. I bought things and began to care about what was in my space in ways I never had before. I learned the difference between a cover and a comforter. I learned what a duvet, a credenza, and an armoire is. I learned of someone named Christopher Lowell and his apparent superstar status among women as the go-to guy for home décor needs.

My apartment did not have a shower, only a bath. So I learned to incorporate in my life the art of intentional care and cleansing. I became a connoisseur of bathing and skin products: my bathroom was full of soaps, exfoliates (a new word learned along the way), and moisturizers. I learned that home was about atmosphere, and that objects in it create a habitable place for mind, body, and soul to dwell. My apartment also did not have a stove or a refrigerator. The landlord offered to put one in but I opted not to since it would save me a hundred bucks a month on rent. I was a bachelor, and my job had me traveling a lot so I wasn't planning on cooking anyway. I had a microwave and my refrigerator from college, and that was fine.

I'm a lonesome, not lonely, person by nature. It's not a fatal condition, but it is chronic, something to medicate when it flares up. My former wife and I only shared one Christmas together. We went to Hawaii, but we barely talked. We argued that trip, an ugly situation in a very beautiful place. The beginning of December always marks an emotional turn for me. Our wedding anniversary is in the beginning of December. The day came and went, and nobody noticed what that day meant except for her and me, and yet we wouldn't hear each other's voice. My first Christmas without her was spent with leftover pizza I'd ordered the night before knowing I wasn't going to leave my apartment the next day. I turned off my phone, ate the pizza, watched television, and slept alone. Every Christmas since then has been the same.

Chicago winters can be long and very cold, and they would bring on a depression that would stay with me for months on end. I was a functional depressive, even while traveling and ministering and caring for others. I'd come home, drop my bags, and sit on the floor for hours, sometimes crying and other times just wondering what was happening in my life. Sometimes there's a state of sadness where tears won't come; it's a space of distilled emptiness. I learned that in Korean theology *haan* connotes a mind or heart's affliction and struggle, with a deep emotional or spiritual pain that either poisons the entire being or ends up nourishing the person. Both were happening to me at the same time and I didn't know it.

I was angry all the time, but no one else knew it. And I didn't understand it myself. I hid my anger from view, but when alone I was flooded with memories and regret. I'd sit for hours and relive moments that we'd shared. Some made me laugh and some deepened my sadness. Anniversaries passed, birthdays passed, holidays passed, good days and bad days passed. We had no communication with one another, and slowly but surely what was once alive in my heart began to die. It's like blowing out a candle. At first you can see the flame go out and smell the extinguishing of the wick, but in a few moments you can't tell if the candle had ever burned hot or given illumination. In my soul, I can remember the moment I divorced her and how it was over. There was nothing to hold onto anymore, there was nothing for me to lose in letting go. I wanted my life to be my own. She didn't know it yet, but I was done, and from that moment on going to court was just a mere formality.

Not Who I Was Anymore

I thought that when I got divorced the pain would be over. I thought that I'd just move on. But it wasn't that simple. I was wounded in ways I had yet to discover. I became sensitive to my pain even if I couldn't name it or understand it. I became sensitive to the pain in others. My religious upbringing had taught me only one thing to do under these circumstances, and that was to pray, pray, and somehow everything would be okay, somehow over the course of time I'd get better. But I wasn't getting better. I was getting worse. I wanted healing for my soul. I needed to be consoled at the deepest core of myself. I became sensitive in ways that made me gravitate toward things that I thought would ease my pain. Everything I tried failed.

There was nothing in my religious background that had trained me to be aware of self and to address what I needed. So I found myself in the arms of paramours trying to piece my manhood and self-esteem back together again. I was needy for love, which made me a slave to it. Wherever I sensed it could be, I allowed my heart to lay there. I often wanted to whisper in the throes of lovemaking, "Do you see me? Do you know how weak I am? Can you understand how broken I feel?" "My heart is trembling from your touch, can you feel that?"

I wanted my lovers to tell me I mattered to them, and my mind got lost in the fantasy of passionate nights with illusionary and vain meanings. Many of them wanted more from me than just a moment, but I had nothing more to give. They were content to touch my body, but they were really reaching for my heart and it wasn't there. Frail and lifeless, I had hidden all that was left of it. I'd hidden it even from myself, not wanting to be hurt by anyone anymore, including me.

When words fail to vent love and passion for someone, love communicates that magnetism through our bodies, expressing nonverbal sentiments just as powerful and clear as the most romantic sonnet. Magnetism is invisible. For it to manifest itself, it must find life through giving. I wish I'd had more to give. I've allowed good women who loved me and wanted to be a part of my life to leave me because they had no sure footing that allowed them to feel safe with me. I wasn't ready to have someone in my life again. I wasn't ready to love.

I thought part of the healing process was to get back on the proverbial horse. It was a bumpy ride on a long trail of tears. I went on a date one night, a simple visit to a dessert bar and a long, slow walk under a clear sky in downtown Chicago. My date and I talked and strolled, sometimes silently, just enjoying each other's company. As I drove her home that night, she touched my hand, putting hers on top of mine as it rested on the gearshift. Her touch was tender, caring, and as sweet as she was.

I walked her to the door, and she went ahead of me as I stopped on the steps of her home. She put the key in the door, turned it slightly, and cracked the door. She then walked back down the steps where I was waiting and came real close to me. She was all of four-foot-eleven in heels, with long wavy hair framing an unblemished almond complexion. She hugged me, burying her face in my chest, and then ever so slightly she looked up at me. Our eyes met. She had the biggest brown, doe-like eyes I'd ever seen. I saw the moon in her eyes that night and the hope she held for us. I saw how much she wanted to be part of my life, and I saw a sweet surrender in her eyes waiting for me to welcome her into my heart.

I knew that look. I'd seen it before. And I knew how vulnerable it could make me feel. I quickly hid my eyes from her and kissed her forehead.

I told her I'd call her later. And we embraced. I walked back to my car knowing what I had to do. I got home, opened my phone, and deleted her number. She would call, and I wouldn't answer the phone. I never saw her again. It wasn't a bad date. She was a beautiful girl, and I could have loved her. But I wasn't ready. I wasn't free.

After that, for over a year, I wouldn't see anyone. I traveled a lot then for my job, which occupied my mind and my time. The trips helped me escape the emptiness I felt at home, where I filled extended periods with fast food, movies, and a body pillow I'd cling to in the middle of the night like a life preserver.

As spring approached, I came out of hibernation. I was not any better spiritually or emotionally, but being alone during the winter had taught me new disciplines. I'd learned to take care of myself. I'd domesticated myself and become something of a neat freak. I had in fact become self-sufficient. I reveled in the feeling of moving from near total dependency on my former wife to not needing her at all.

I've committed many emotional transgressions in my life, and as I replay them, I'm often reminded of a passage from William Shakespeare: "Such is my love, to thee I so belong, that for thy right I will bear all wrong."

Octavia's Love

Springtime in Chicago has always been special for me, the season of new things to cherish about the city I love. After long cold winter nights the city emerges in spontaneously curious ways that not only warm the air but the soul. Near the end of spring, after the first winter of my separation, I met Octavia.

I remember her like it was yesterday. We met casually through a mutual friend at a community revitalization function. We briefly made small talk and at the end of the evening I walked her to her car. Something in her voice made me feel safe. That night I told Octavia I was divorced recently, and she told me that she was sorry to hear that.

"I feel terrible for you, can I help?" She asked, seeming to genuinely care. This was what I needed most and what I hadn't had in a long time. I so appreciated the concern in her voice, it stayed with me for days. We exchanged numbers, and the next day I called her for no specific reason. She never asked me why I called. Maybe she knew. Perhaps intuitively she understood what my words could not convey. Maybe she understood that I was reaching out, and she allowed me to. Our conversations soon slipped into an oddly familiar place as if it were completely normal. It was like we'd spent a lifetime talking to one another. We talked on the phone, and I was unusually open with her after having been imprisoned by a closed heart for so long. I wanted to talk, and I needed someone to listen.

Women often complain that men don't talk. But we do and Octavia talked to me as if she had read a how-to manual. She knew how not to force conversation. She knew how to listen. She seduced me by first asking me, "How was your day?" Her genuine curiosity and attention to me made me want to talk to her more. When men talk with women, it must be more than the exchange of information and gripes. I wanted to talk to her because I loved her laugh. I hadn't laughed about silly things with a woman in years. I wanted to talk with her because she thought I was funny, and I enjoyed being silly with her. I began to adore her.

I wanted to talk and I wanted to talk with her. I wanted her to know where I was in my life. Her maternal instincts were profound and peaceful. After a rough day, Octavia was for me the one place where I could find calmness and rest. I traveled a lot at the time for work so we did not see each other for another few weeks, but it was amazing how close we became in such a short length of time. She gave me the companionship I was missing. When I was home, she made herself available to me in small ways that I didn't take for granted. She dignified my heart with her presence and her care. She was there for me and, though I never told her, I was falling in love again. We'd do incredibly simple things like grocery shopping. She'd ride with me to run small, mundane errands. When I was away, she'd help with some of the small things that I couldn't do. She cared for me, and for those moments the pain of being divorced and lonely was minimized. I felt so loved.

I hadn't felt cared for and important to a woman in years. It was healing and scary at the same time. I felt my heart being resuscitated by her presence and life seemed a little lighter. And yet I was quietly panicking because I felt myself falling emotionally in a way I promised I never would again. I felt special and wanted again. I felt alive again. She made me feel valuable. I didn't know how much I'd missed those feelings. I began to love her deeply and we began a very passionate physical relationship. Our togetherness was intoxicating and overwhelming. She possessed me in a loving and fulfilling way that was so different, so real, and so vivid. Everything about her was a song of perfection: the smell of her hair, the softness of her lips, the taste of her neck, the sound of her voice, the smoothness of her skin. Her femininity was divine, and being with her brought a joy that had eluded me for a very long time.

Time moved in a different way when we were together. My heart pounded faster, but time moved achingly slower. It never seemed like enough time when we were together, but at a point each time I held her I knew it could be the final time, for somewhere in my heart I knew that this wouldn't last and that this goodbye would be terrible for both of us. It was as if we'd been in love before in a past life. It's amazing how a love can feel so right and yet be so wrong.

As I've gotten older, I respect and appreciate time. Not just being on time for meetings and the like, but that there's a time for things to happen and for certain things to be. There's a time to love and to embrace, and there's a time to hate and a time to refrain from embracing. The reality is that sometimes we can have a right love at the wrong time in our lives, which can create pain that does not easily subside.

I wrestled with what I knew was the truth, and the truth was that I could not keep her in my life. I had to say goodbye. The truth is I wasn't ready yet. She never knew the internal struggle that I was having. She never knew that certain things she did with sincerity triggered an emotional paralysis for me. I was holding onto her, still not knowing who I was because I hadn't done the work to free myself of my past, and her love wasn't strong enough to reconstruct things that life and love had destroyed in me. I was still a shell of a man coming up on thirty years old, and I found myself becoming needy and dependent on her in ways that were not healthy. I was still angry. I held her some nights wishing she was my ex-wife. I was still walking into crowded rooms looking to see if Denae was there. I was still reliving the past. I was in love with Octavia but I never told her because I wasn't free and the words just wouldn't come. I battled with what I knew was right and what I felt in my heart. What I felt was killing me. So we said a very sad and tearful goodbye.

It was painful for me because I finally had a love that was nurturing and fulfilling, and yet all of me had not been put back together so that I could give her what she needed from me. I didn't trust God to give me another relationship that would be as fulfilling as that one, which is why I wrestled to keep it. I was afraid to have it and afraid to let it go. So I found a place of peace and I let what was going to happen, happen. Success in life is forwarded in the moment we let it happen.

We parted ways and she thought it would be best that we not see each other anymore. I understood but I thought of her a lot. Women rarely understand how difficult it is for a man to leave a relationship. Sometimes saying goodbye when we don't want to is the most responsible and merciful thing to do. I was experiencing yet another relationship loss. Looking over my shoulder, I understand now that the Creator sometimes takes what's wrong and uses it as a tool to help us discover our way and become who we should be.

After a lot of talking, Octavia and I eventually moved on, and it was for the best. She's married now and currently expecting her second child. Every love story doesn't have a happy ending, and I'm mature enough not to demand that of life. I miss her painfully sometimes, but often life is about sacrificing things you'd rather keep so someone else can be free.

The Brokenhearted

Where do broken hearts go? I've broken more than my fair share and I've had my heart broken at least as many times. I also know what it feels like to have someone walk away from you without much explanation. To love is to risk, and there's no safe way to love. What hindered my development was that my definition of love was very narrow and incomplete, coupled with the fact that I thought love could only live in a certain context. I have in the past thought love was synonymous with pleasure. It was only through much searching spiritually and intellectually that I discovered that's not true at all. There's a duality to love — it encompasses an element of pain and pleasure. I got married thinking that love was supposed to always feel good. Since it didn't, I questioned if she loved me or if I loved her.

The Creator is the only one who can balance what we receive from love in life. Love is a Herculean feat within itself. Love is durable and stubborn. The pain of bad relationships breaks us in ways that are many times too painful to express in words. Yet God is able to heal us and free us from our past. As I've gotten older, I've done some things I said I'd never do, and gone places I said I'd never go.

My breakup with Octavia left me more fragmented than before we met. I became bitter and cynical and more withdrawn. At the time, one of my best friends and I started a practice of sitting down and talking once a week to catch up, talk about books and life. One night he noticed that I was unusually disheveled, and watching my behavior over some weeks he recognized that my mental health was deteriorating.

A Golden Moment

"You should think about getting some professional help," he told me. "You aren't getting better and I'm concerned." I thought about it for a second and responded by saying, "Okay, sure."

He was right, I wasn't getting better and I knew it. The more I tried to untangle myself the more entangled I became. I was caught in a very complex web, and didn't want to spend the next sixty-five years tied up with something that happened in my twenties. He recommended a therapist, and I made an appointment. Without question, that was one of the most important decisions I've ever made in my life. To choose a therapeutic course as a companion to my spiritual transformation has helped me unearth issues that I purposely forgot and helped me rediscover and reclaim who I am.

A lot has been written about black men and mental health. In America we're the least likely of all social groups to seek therapy but we're the most vulnerable to mental and emotional abuse.

As humans we're all prone to mental infirmities, and the help we need does not come by prayer alone. I was eager to begin the process. I wasn't nervous or afraid, but I quickly realized how much I was in denial and couldn't be honest with myself. I was retelling stories, protecting people, and blaming myself for things that were done to me.

"If you're not going to be honest, then don't come back" the therapist said abruptly. She was right, but I was so conditioned to do damage control on my pain and justify violations and abuses that had occurred in my life that I didn't know how to turn that off and be transparent. Gradually, I was given tools that help me reconnect with my divine self. I learned what it meant to be faithful to myself through mercy, grace, and forgiveness. And I learned not to fear goodbyes and how to have the courage to say hello again.

Part Two

CHAPTER V

Changed by Night

I never know what to expect from love...

It was 2 AM and I received a call from the church's answering service about midnight; they relayed a message to call a member at the hospital. Upon doing so, I learned that a couple's newborn child had passed away. I gathered my belongings and went from my home into a humid summer Chicago night. On the fifteen-minute drive to the hospital I meditated on what to expect and tried to visualize what I might encounter, pulling on case studies and the like to deal with not death alone but the complicated subtext that often accompanies death.

I had read and was as prepared as I thought I could be. By now I'd learned that words aren't always the most meaningful gift you can give at such times; mostly, it's just your presence and emotional support that matters most. My canned answers and clichés often seem cheap and not at all life-giving. I keenly posses the ability to be intuitive about delicate situations, so I was confident that when I got to the hospital I could assess the situation and know what gifts I needed to lean on to bring support to the family. I've learned to see hospitals as places of healing, and in some cases a safe place to die. I'm always aware that within this one context are very polarizing forces, life and death. Both are important to how we understand ourselves.

It's amazing to me how still and quiet a hospital can be at night. As I walked alone through the various corridors to reach the waiting family I heard the click of my shoes bouncing off the walls. The echoes make me nervous. It feels like my steps are too heavy and loud, which makes me self-conscious about my stride. I try to soften my steps so as not to disturb the quietness that I figure must be essential for the nighttime staff, but it doesn't work. There's a scent in the air, which reminds me of my early hospital stays as a child, or the hundreds of times I've gone through hospital doors. The scent awakens memories that distract from my nervousness.

I finally get to the desk and introduce myself. "I am Pastor Shaffer. I'm here for the Nelson family. Where can I find them?" The nurse points me down an empty corridor that leads to a door. As I walk through the door I'm greeted by another nurse who's standing outside the family room. She informs me that the family is waiting. My prejudices about the situation had led me to mentally play out how this encounter would go.

I was ready to hear the story that would be filled with how's and why's. I was prepared to hug all those who may have needed an embrace of comfort, to console all those that there is a tomorrow, and with tomorrow there's hope for more peace and happiness. I was prepared to pray with the family.

But what I discovered as I walked into that room changed me and is still very much alive in me. As I moved closer to the room where the family was, the father of the child greeted me. His eyes seem weary and troubled, which was to be expected. But in his eyes I discerned something more. In his eyes was fear, the kind of fear that leaves you numb to anything around you. His breathing was short but not heavy.

Before we said a word to each other I reached out my hand to his, and put my other hand on his shoulder. He was trembling. His voice was there but it was not strong. I asked what exactly happened with the baby. He told me that the child was born three and a half months premature, and that the lungs and other internal organs had not developed to the point where the child could independently breathe and get stronger. Over the last three months the baby had endured more than ten operations and procedures to buy more time for the child. He ultimately passed away from respiratory failure. His little under-developed lungs wouldn't allow him to take in enough air to breathe normally.

The doctor, who I know had seen more than his fair share of death, seemed genuinely moved, and stayed with us as we talked. The baby had endured until he had no more fight in him. The father explained to me that he and his wife had not been married long and that, while he had children from a previous marriage, this was her first child. He went on to say what a miracle it was for his wife because for years the doctors told her that she'd never be able to conceive. My heart ached for them and for the grief they felt. After our conversation, I asked him where his wife was. He turned around slightly and gestured me to follow him.

I walked into the room and found his wife sitting in the corner holding something. Holding something as if she was protecting it or hiding it. What she held was close to her chest and rose to her face. I called out to her and my calling to her did not faze her. She did not look up or acknowledge my presence. I moved closer and sat next to her. I peered in and moved closer still to discover that she was holding the dead child in her arms. My gaze was fixed upon this child, who had half-opened eyes, purplish puffy cheeks and a swollen face, no doubt because of the entire trauma this infant body had been through. I saw a tiny hand poking out from the blanket as if reaching for a finger to grab, but the small hand was still.

I sat down next to her, not to disturb her but to better understand what exactly was happening. For the next fifteen minutes, as I sat beside her saying nothing, she sang lullabies to the baby. I heard her tell the baby that she had a beautiful room for him with lots of toys and gifts that her friends had sent. "The doctors say mommy can take you home now, you're all better," she whispered to him. "Your room is all painted for you; your name is painted on the wall in your favorite color."

"Jessica," I called out quietly to her. She looked up at me, eyes red and puffy from tears that affirmed her pain and love for her child. "It's Pastor Shaffer. Do you know where you are?" She nodded slowly. "Can I hold the baby? I won't go anywhere. I'll be right here." She stood and placed the child in my waiting arms. The child was heavy as I clutched him. "He's a beautiful baby, isn't he, Pastor?" She said with an innocent half-smile. "Yes he is, a beautiful baby boy," I replied.

It was obvious that the love she had for her child refused to allow her mind to grasp that her child was dead. Love is stubborn and unyielding even in the face of death itself. Love is perhaps the most resistant force on earth; it marches on regardless of wounds. Through disaster and disappointments Love shoulders its load and still climbs the steepest mountain toward its own summit.

In that moment my mind and heart hit a wall. The sorrow I felt for her was beyond what I had the capacity to comprehend. I was heartbroken for her and her dreams of being a mother. "Wait here a moment. The doctor wants to see the baby, okay?" "Okay, I'll wait right here. I'm not going anywhere because I'm taking the baby home tonight," she said.

I stepped away with the baby in my arms to confer with the doctor and her husband. We talked about how to bring this grieving mother into consciousness and be there to support her when the sheer force of her love crashes against the reality of living life without what she felt she deserved. Every love story doesn't have a happy ending but love is not lessened when it's not forever. Sometimes the mere fact that we had love to give is a miracle all within itself.

I drove away from the hospital that night changed in very profound ways.

CHAPTER VI

Rest Well ...

There is restless rest in love that lulls our hearts into a peaceful place beyond understanding. It is where we are fully embraced by the divine.

I'm a church kid, in every sense of the word. I can never remember a time when I was not in church. We went to church for everything and for nothing. Church was not just a spiritual center, it was for us an extension of our family. I wanted to go to church because I had cousins, aunts, friends who became part of my early childhood existence. My memories are blessed by wonderful thoughts of joyous times shared in church and after church, in fellowship halls and at the homes of friends.

I'm grateful that God has kept me by grace alone. As I look over my shoulder, I've seen a falling away of my peers. I call them "church casualties." Boys and girls who didn't survive the ups and downs that come with being part of an imperfect sacred society called the black church. They could not on some level process the hypocrisy and the idiosyncratic nature of the church and ultimately left the church and God altogether.

They left injured and bleeding, falling into a world that ravaged what was left of their wounded hearts. Some have fallen away from the faith that was instilled in them as children, and some have fallen on very hard times, leading to drug addiction, jail, and death. Some of the comrades of my naive childhood have died in drug deals gone fatally wrong, became enslaved to drug addiction, and infected with HIV/AIDS because at some point the church didn't react responsibly to the issues that they carried in their hearts that ultimately led to bad and sometimes regrettably fatal behaviors in their lives.

I haven't forgotten them and mourn them deeply now. I've carried them in my heart to remind me that every person is a child of God and each one is an expression of God's love. No matter how broken or the depth of failing, the ever-present force of love still seeks to be known by them, whether gay, straight, drug addicted, or alcoholic, they all matter. Since they matter to God, then as I am a vessel of God's mercy and grace, they matter to me also and unapologetically so.

I am an idealist and believe that no matter what we are or what we are not, at the time of our own choosing we can become who we were meant to be. If we commit to our choices and summon enough bravery to look at ourselves as we are and be challenged by what we are not, then we can find a way to recalibrate ourselves to be a useful tool in God's plan for our lives.

What I am not, however, is an ideological purist. As a church leader, I do not feel compelled to replicate the church in a way that is not conducive to the expression of God's love for everyone. It would've been easier for me to upload a viable template of church that is at once historic and predictable. But my sometimes petulant and mostly creative nature wouldn't allow me to live in the pastorate in any other way than the way I do now. Like Michelangelo or Picasso, I'm in love with the blank canvas, for in it I'm enticed by the vividness of its possibilities and potentials.

This has been costly, when you think out loud and dare reconsider sacred community assumptions, ideas, and paradigms that have been long held and worshipped. If I show that widely held assumptions may be consistently ineffective, that sets you up for criticism even if you make sense. While we should never turn a deaf ear to criticism, we must be challenged by it to go deeper in reflection and still make headway with new ideas and ways of thinking that must emerge if the church is to progress.

"Pastor, I didn't agree with what you said in your sermon last week," a member said respectfully. I responded in kind by saying, "I'm glad you didn't. Let's talk about it and maybe we can both learn something." It's hard for me to figure out exactly where we got the idea that you had to agree with everything your pastor said or that your pastor has to embody your ideals about every social, political, or spiritual issue, or every concern of the day. That's an impossible and unreasonable assumption that denies us the possibility to create teachable moments from faithful dissents within our congregations.

November 6, 2005, 7:45 AM

The night before our first church service I stayed up the night before. I was still wrestling with all the cataclysmic changes that were happening in my life, trying to find a glimmer of peace through all the things that were shifting. There are moments that we chase throughout our lives, events maybe that before they even occur we've ascribed great meaning to. As our imagination expands, those moments deepen and add to how we define ourselves.

I've had other moments that I had anticipated and was excited to see come. But quite honestly they never lived up to how I'd defined them in my head or heart. They always left me wanting and keenly aware of how empty the experience was. Now I found myself at a moment I'd anticipated for well over ten years, and while I was happy there was also a profound emptiness that couldn't be ignored. Looking over my shoulder, I see the wisdom of God hidden in choices I made and choices that were made for me.

What forced me into the full throne senior pastorate was being fired after five years by my boss, a once-prominent church leader. The worst of it was that he notified me by email. In hindsight it was the best thing that could have happened to me. Along with the undignified way I was let go, I also felt betrayed. I thought the bond we had forged over the years made us closer than what had become of our relationship and after looking up to him for some time, I was left with a final act of what I saw to be a classless act of cowardice. But, I was free.

Liberation is expensive but it's well worth the price. God in one moment was bringing people into my life and taking people out of my life, and I didn't know how to feel. On one hand I was sad because

I was losing things I would've wanted to keep. I wanted to grow but I also wanted things to stay the same, I wanted to move but I also wanted to stay in the same place, and that was not possible. I had to walk by faith, not knowing who was going to come with me and what was going to happen.

Our first service lasted all of twenty-five minutes. We had worship, I led the sacrament of communion, and I preached. We didn't have a choir and the only announcement was, please come back next week. We had members when we started, a faithful bunch out of which the majority are still with us, but I told my grandmother the night before service that if I opened the doors of the church and she saw that no one moved she was suppose to come so I wouldn't look silly waiting for people to join.

Well, I did open the doors for membership and asked everyone to bow their heads while people reflect on the choice they may need to make. While their heads were bowed, I looked at my grandmother, trying to signal her that she was supposed to come up. But she'd put her head down with everybody else, so I pondered that if I threw my Bible at her, she'd lift her head and come down.

I decided against that because we would have been found out. Also, I didn't want anybody to misread me flinging my Bible across the room at an old lady who happened to be my grandmother. Later that night at her house, I sat next to her on her bed, looked her in the eye, and said, "We will never make it in Vegas unless we rehearse more."

Got to Be Me

I've learned to be in communication with my own heart. Aloneness and stillness are great tools to help us locate the most sincere and tender parts of ourselves. When we're left alone we can hear clearly our own voice and begin to discern that maybe how we speak, how we live, and the expression of life that we project is not our true selves but maybe a caricature of what other people want us to be.

Confusion comes when the ethics of being and the ethics of doing are in different places and we haven't been allowed the space to know ourselves. When we act like people want us to act and make choices that are in the best interest of other parties — while denying our inner compass — what we are and what we do come in conflict with one another. The integration of the parts of self that have been scattered along the roads of our lives at some point must be collected if we're to ever find the wholeness that allows us to live in a whole and transparent relationship with God that frees our souls to love someone else, that frees ourselves to be with other people with a sense of self-awareness that's necessary to sustain fulfilling commitments.

After some time I started getting feedback telling me I should change my style. I felt like people wanted me to holler or tap dance or do something showy. But to do those things would not allow me to be true to myself. I knew that being anyone else would cause me to fail quickly and if I had to do that to be popular or "successful," I'd rather not do it at all.

The prevailing thought was that nobody's going to come hear me lecture every week, so I did try for a minute, with disastrous results. For a couple of weeks I tried to whoop and close out my messages strong. The only problem was that at the time I was in the midst of a sinus infection, so to remedy that I took some Benadryl before service so that by the time I had to close the message, I'd have clear sinuses. Well, where I was preaching there was a vent for the air conditioning over my head, so I was sweating and preaching, and the air stopped my sinuses up because it was blowing right above me. So when the Benadryl kicked in, I started hearing voices in my head. The conversation went like this:

> Self: Can you breathe right now?
> Me: No
> Self: Do you have a nurse here?
> Me: No
> Self: Do they have an oxygen tank just in case you pass out?

Me: No.

Self: Okay, then maybe you need to stop this foolishness and go sit down somewhere.

Me: I think so too.

So I stopped in the midst of my Benadryl-hazed preaching. Usually after service, someone will say "Pastor, you did a great job today with the message." Someone may have said that, I just don't remember. The lesson I learned was twofold: one, do not medicate yourself when you have to preach or do any type of public speaking, and two, simply be yourself.

Our lives are sometimes filled with "lost loves." Love moments that slip out of our hands when we thought we had a good grip. Grief is the price we pay when we choose to love someone or when love chooses us.

Mother Mary

"Okay, get some rest and I'll see you later," I said. "Okay," she replied, "you too, Pastor." I kissed her cheek and turned to walk away. That was the end of our last conversation.

Mother Mary Wiggins was one of two church Mothers we had at our still brand-new community. Our church was a little more than three years old at the time, and most times I felt like I was keeping things together with duct tape and crazy glue. Caring for this community has been the hardest and the most fulfilling thing I've done in my life. I feel every movement, whether it's a step forward, a stumble, or a step backward. There've been moments where I've given my best and realized that my best wasn't good enough, and there've been moments when I thought my investments weren't enough and watched as grace made my little more than enough.

Our church is small and cozy. There's a peace with small things that I appreciate, and it nurtures closeness between people. Lives and loves are shared when people come together around common goals and I've so enjoyed being a part of this community. I've had to keep my heart from envy as I look over my shoulder with amazement at what some of the peers have accomplished. I've kept from defining my worth based on how many people I see at church each week. I have not pushed for our church to be more just for the sake of being more, and to insulate inherent insecurities. I medicated my angst in some moments by being patient in knowing that faithfulness and consistency are the true marks of success in any field.

In intimate moments we share as a community is where great but tiny seeds of destiny are nurtured. Mother Wiggins along with her family became members of the City of Faith family when we were about three or four months old. I love old people and gravitated toward and loved her immediately. I think it's because of her wisdom and her perspectives on life. I respect someone who has lived a long time, has been in church, and has "been there and done that," yet makes a decision to hear me ramble from week to week about God and the meaning of life. Its affirming in ways that I'm not able to articulate with enough grace to express my love and appreciation for dignifying my life with her presence.

I revere the kindness and love she showed me. I intend not to let down her or any of our members. She had any number of health challenges, like older people do, and we'd talk about her care and what she was doing to get better, and the things she wasn't doing to get better. I always asked because I cared. It bothers me when I see people I love in pain, it moves me to want to help even when I know ultimately it's not up to me and there's very little I can do. She'd be in pain and I knew it, but she wouldn't tell me. She knew I worried about her and I appreciated her being protective of my feelings.

On this particular Sunday I had an altar call. I felt led to touch the members to confer blessings upon their lives. Usually I'd have to wrestle and put her in a headlock to pray for her, but unusually that day she came spontaneously. I remember touching her head and felt a peace pass between us, but thought nothing of it. The service progressed, and on this particular Sunday I preached on the subject

LOVE AGAIN

"God's Promise of Rest," from the book of Hebrews, chapter four. Service was over and we stood in the lobby, talking on a warm Chicago afternoon about her travels and changing her medication to coincide with her schedule.

"Mother, I had a dream you fixed a peach cobbler for me and brought it to church next Sunday," I said with an impish smile as I put my arm around her. "What size was the peach cobbler in your dream, Pastor?" she said with a half smile, half frown. "A really big one!" I responded quickly, and we both laughed.

"Okay, get some rest and I'll see you later," I said. "Okay," she replied, "you too, Pastor." I kissed her cheek and turned to walk away.

After Sunday service I have a custom: either I'm going to go home and take a nap or, because of left-over energy, I'll go to the gym to unwind. This Sunday I went straight to bed. I hate to hear the phone ring so most times it's on vibrate or silent. When I rolled over mid-afternoon I knew something was wrong because I had about twenty missed calls. Alarmed, I returned one of the calls and was informed that Mother Wiggins had collapsed at home and soon passed away. "Okay, where are you? I'll be right there." I called my brother as I threw on some clothes and rushed to the hospital in a daze, eyes wide with amazement. I was dumbfounded and confused. I rolled down the windows so I could feel the air on my face. I walked into the hospital to be met by grief-stricken family and friends. "She's gone, Pastor," said her daughter as she hugged me tight.

I'm a professional and this is my vocation. I'm trained to deal with these situations in theory, but one of the ones whom I cared for and who had allowed me to be her pastor, one whom I loved, had left me.

I gathered the family and friends in the room with her remains and we prayed and thanked God for sharing this warm soul with us for these moments, and we asked God to give us strength in this time of pain.

I left the hospital and was a mixture of emotions that even now are very hard to describe. "I just saw her, we just talked how she could be gone," I said to myself as I drove home.

That night my anger was visceral and I was angry with God. I prayed that night: You have got to be kidding me. Are you serious? I'm out here doing what you called me to do and this is what I get for it? I'm all by myself trying to be faithful to you and this church. How could you take her from me? I don't have that many members as it is. I can't believe you'd do this to me, not now, not when I'm barely able to get my head above water. The least you could do is keep them alive!

I said many more things that night as I threw a tantrum of monumental proportions. I cried myself to sleep and woke up with the sun shining through my windows and a soft breeze filling my room. I felt God with me. I'd need that presence in the days to come.

I was livid. The coming week would be the most painful and humbling time I would ever see. It so happened that our church rents space and there was an event planned for the day we needed to have the service. So I asked around the area to see if any church would be hospitable and open their doors for us. Some of them said flatly no, others said they couldn't do it for one reason or another. I went and asked a prominent church on the South Side if it would open its doors so I could celebrate the life of our beloved mother. They said no because it's their church policy not to have funerals on Saturdays. Having worked full-time in ministry before I pastored, I understood church policy. But I also knew that there are exceptions made when policy needs to be amended. These people were rude and mean. It was humiliating to have to beg, but my love for her humbled me and ultimately I got the yes I needed.

The day of the service was overcast. I was nervous but couldn't grieve. I had to go to work and had to make sure that things would run smoothly. As we ended the hour of visitation and it was time to start the service, my older brother, who is a confidant and friend, stood with me as I began to fold the casket cover and gently folded the edges of the inlay cover, slowly tucking her away for a long and overdue rest.

As I brought the cover over her face, I whispered, "Okay, get some rest. I'll see you later." In reflection tears welled in my eyes, a knot became lodged in my throat, and the pit of my stomach sank all at once as I reached up in finality to close this casket. I knew on an intuitive level that I was closing and burying a small piece of myself with her that day. As days became weeks I found myself crying at the oddest times at the thought of her absence and my own feelings of loss and sadness, but I had very little time to grieve because we had Bible study in a couple of days, and then there was next Sunday — and the cycle continues.

"You cannot conceive, nor can I, of the appalling strangeness of the mercy of God," says Graham Greene. The strangest thing of all though, is that death has not stopped me from being her pastor. Love doesn't recognize graves. The love that lives in our hearts has found a place where death does not reign, for the last enemy that was conquered by Christ was death itself.

CHAPTER VII

When Goodbye Is the Last Thing We Say

When love says hello, I know love. When love says goodbye, I see love. When I lose love, love still has me. I am possessed by love...

Tuesday, May 16, 2008
6:12 AM: Wake up
6:14 AM: Turn on TV to MSNBC
6:20 AM: Brush Teeth
6:36 AM: Drink coffee (I usually don't do this)
7:00 AM: Check e-mail

The message from one of my church members was short and to the point. "I am writing to inform you that I will no longer be attending City of Faith," it said. Maybe I shouldn't have had that cup of coffee. But I was not surprised by the parishioner's decision. In fact, I'd discerned that it was coming long before receiving the e-mail. I knew then as I know now that the church is a transitional institution. People were leaving church long before I started pastoring my congregation, so I'm okay with them going.

However, knowing theoretically that people would leave my congregation is one thing. Experiencing it is quite another. I feel it. It stings. When it happens, I must remind myself that the Church is Christ's bride and I am merely a steward of this congregation. This means that I must maintain a healthy emotional detachment. I will not be an effective leader if I go into depression every time someone decides to leave. But I do care and care deeply. As a pastor, I enjoy watching people grow, even when they grow away from me and our congregation. But I feel the void. It's in this empty emotional state that I've begun to know a very unique grace that comes from God alone. This moment for me is about goodbye.

I've said more than my fair share of goodbyes in my life. Sometimes I've had to say it when it was absolutely necessary for both of us. Sometimes I said it when I didn't want to, but it was the right thing to do. Even when it's the most responsible thing to do, it hurts. Hearts and lives, when in community and harmony, leave great impressions on our souls that cannot and should not be erased. I've embraced this truth: Goodbyes are a part of life and an undeniable part of mine.

From Gladys Knight's "Neither One of Us" to Guy's "Goodbye Love," many writers and poets have given melody to the painful idea of saying goodbye. Maybe they thought if we could hum an infectious tune, our pain would be more bearable. Thank you all, but it was not. However, many times when I remember the loss of love in my life, I'll find some sad song that sums up what I'm feeling at the moment. I suppose it's the masochist in me. I've often listened to Brian McKnight say, "Now I sit all alone wishing all my feelings were gone." Goodbyes don't always end well, but we're often left wishing they did.

We spend our lives living in fear of having to say goodbye or someone close saying it to us. We are innately more comfortable saying hello. There is something unnatural about saying goodbye. Hello is generally synonymous with hope and optimism. When we say hello, we never think that we might one day have to say goodbye.

Death is the ultimate goodbye. It's perplexing and always throws us off balance because we never get used to it. It's painful to stand over an open grave and think to yourself, "I wasn't ready to say goodbye yet." One philosopher said that "grief is the price we pay for love." Death can be cruel, but it's the one goodbye we cannot avoid. As the time neared for Jesus' inevitable departure from the earth, he had one last meal with his beloved disciples. John writes that "having loved his own which were in the world, he loved them unto the end." Jesus knew when he met Peter, James, and John that he would one day have to say goodbye to them. I guess none of us ever escapes the grip of goodbye.

Never Can Say Goodbye

Doing what I do, I get a chance to meet a lot of different people in many different and sometimes strange circumstances.

At the church where I worked before my present ministry, I remember meeting a man named Derek Timmons, who changed my life in a most profound way. He was bald and he appeared to be an older aging man but was only 43 years old. You could see in his eyes that he'd had a hard life and had grown quite weary of it. He joined the church and became a full-fledged member. He was a kind, gentle soul, excited about church life, and I was happy to see the renewed light in his eyes. He was constantly asking about scripture and how he could become more involved in the church. He worked in men's ministry, mentoring, and church security. At times, his enthusiasm bordered on nuisance, but it was a sweet nuisance. And I never hesitated to spend time with him.

A while after joining the church, Derek contracted a fatal respiratory infection. When I went to see him at the hospital, there was a hazard sign outside his door warning visitors to wear a safety mask. Discussing hospital visitations, a church member suggested that in such cases it was best not to wear the mask to avoid alarming the patient about seriousness of his condition. She said it would also make the patient feel better to know a visitor cared enough not to wear the mask.

I don't know whether it was caring or careless not to wear the mask, but I didn't. I walked in and saw Derek wearing an oxygen mask. When he saw me, you wouldn't believe the relief that swept over his tired, gaunt face. It was hard for him to breathe, and I didn't want him to talk too much. I told him he'd get well and be okay. He lifted the mask and said thank you. I touched his head and told him I'd check on him later. The previous time I visited him, he was actually doing better. He still needed oxygen but was getting stronger. We walked the halls and talked. As I was wrapping up the visit, the nurse said he was going to be able to go home. He would just need an oxygen tank.

At the church, we had a benevolence committee to help members in crisis after disasters or death or with medical supplies. They could apply for assistance; depending on availability of funds, we'd provide what help we could. I figured breathing is important and decided to fill out the paperwork and push it through for Derek's oxygen tank. The last time I visited him I told him what I had done. That was on a Tuesday.

On Wednesday morning, he called a couple of times and I told him we were still processing his application. By Wednesday afternoon, we had approval and I went to get his check. He called again several times that afternoon, but I didn't return his calls. I decided instead to wait until Thursday morning. I would call him, purchase the tank and other supplies, and take him home.

Thursday morning I went into the church office, and the office manager had a strange look on her face.

"What's going on?" I asked

"The hospital called about Derek," she said.

"Okay, I got the check. I'll take it over now."

"No wait," she said. "He passed away."

My heart sunk. The office manager asked if I was okay. I mumbled something and went into my office. On my desk was the pink telephone message slip saying that Derek had called at 4:30 PM on Wednesday, the day before. I cried because I hadn't called him back. I was going to, but I didn't. I wasn't ignoring him. I just wanted to wait until I had the check in hand before I talked to him. In my head, I know that my calling him back would not have added one more second to his life. I know that. But in my heart, I think what is still so painful is that I fear in his last moments of life he may have felt like I didn't care enough to call him back. I don't know.

I sat guilt-ridden at the funeral. I viewed his body, struggling to hold back tears because I didn't want anybody brought in on my grief. I remember standing alone at his open casket mumbling, "I am so sorry. I am so sorry. I am so sorry." In cases like this I didn't usually go to the gravesite, but this time I did. I felt like I needed to go. I did the committal and waited for everybody to leave as they lowered his body into the ground.

That was six or seven years ago. I still have the pink message note tucked inside his obituary. Periodically, I abuse myself as I look at it and relive all those guilt-ridden memories. It's not always easy letting go. Sometimes it takes much longer than we want. Maybe it's a reflection of how I feel about all my relationships — that it was my fault. What could I have done to fix it? Was there something more I could've done? Could I have said something? I have no answers. But it doesn't stop me from asking the questions.

Derek's death wasn't the first or the last time I felt that way. I had an aunt named Maureen. We called her "Aunt Mo." I loved her. She was a tall woman, an energetic five feet ten inches and as tough as any man. She was a pistol, but also very sweet. She had two boys, and went through some pretty rough times, including a nasty divorce.

Some years ago, her health started failing, and she was in and out of hospitals with everything from kidney failure to breast cancer. My older brother and I visited her a few times in the hospital and talked to each other and to her about donating a kidney. We would've done it without a second thought because she was someone who'd been with us at graduations, birthdays, and so many other special occasions. Now that she was bedridden with sores, hair gone from chemotherapy, teeth gone, just withering away, we felt it was the least we could do.

On a bright sunny afternoon after I'd been divorced about a year and half, I went to talk with her. I knew in my heart it would be the last time I'd ever speak with her. We talked about life and love and how she wanted the best for me. She was confident that I'd find somebody to be happy with again, and because she said it, I believed it. I didn't mind being open and vulnerable talking with her.

"I don't know if I can ever recover," I told her. "It still hurts a lot. I feel betrayed, and I don't know if I can get over that."

She was as reassuring as she could be, talking during her therapy sessions. When we returned to her room, she was tired from trying to stay up and talk to me. I knew I was being selfish, but I just didn't want to leave her. We also talked about death that day, and the fact that she was going to leave. We talked about things that caused us to misunderstand each other, she apologized and so did I. She said she loved me and that she wasn't afraid to die. Her will was so strong. She was just staying around because she loved her children and her grandchildren. I told her it was okay and that she didn't have to stay around for us if she was tired. "It's okay to go to sleep," I said. I held her arm for a while, and she fell asleep. I left the hospital that day knowing I wouldn't talk to her again. I learned how to live watching her die that day. Death is inevitable, but so is life and so is love.

Matters of the Heart

I have committed many emotional transgressions in the name of love. Many times the biggest mistake was welcoming someone into my life knowing that eventually there would have to be a painful goodbye. I knew it intuitively but ignored it to play out a fantasy fueled by my loneliness and pain.

God is the only one who can balance what we receive from love. Loving again is a Herculean feat within itself. Love is durable and stubborn. The pain of bad relationships breaks us in ways that can be too painful to describe in words, yet God is able to heal us and free us from our past. As I've gotten older, I've done some things I said I'd never do, and gone places I said I'd never go. But through it all, I've found new reasons to love God, and that love fills so many voids in my life. He gives me the confidence and the faith I need to get out of bed and to let out all the gifts and graces that live in me. So when goodbye must be said, always know that as we live out our days, we must be courageous enough to say, "Hello" once again.

CHAPTER VIII

Love, No Limit

Love knows me, and I know love.

"Goodnight mommy," I said as I kissed her cheek and scurried up to my room where my brother Nash was sleeping already. I was seven and he was nine, and we shared just about everything, including a bedroom.

I was still awake a full hour after kissing my mother goodnight. I can't remember why. Maybe it was the aroma of fresh baked cookies cooling in the kitchen. I was taking them to school in the morning as my bake sale contribution.

My seven-year-old mind easily rationalized that I needed to taste-test them to make sure they'd be good. I slipped out of bed and tiptoed downstairs ever so quietly. I knew every creak in every step and made sure to avoid them. I made it down the steps into the dark living room in silence, careful not to bump anything that would make noise and wake my parents. Usually there were night-lights throughout the house, but they weren't on this night. I was wearing classic 1980s feet pajamas that made a scratching sound because of the plastic soles. As I slowly moved closer to the kitchen, it seemed warmer than usual, and I was warmer than I should've been.

I inched my way along the wall that led to the kitchen and saw a huge, amber light shining on the entire wall. It was beautiful, but as I stared at the flickering light, I suddenly realized it was fire. Our house was on fire!

I remembered from school what to do in case of a fire. I was supposed to stop, drop, and roll. I did, but not before grabbing a handful of cookies. I tucked them away in my pockets, stopped in the middle of the burning kitchen, dropped to the floor and rolled into the living room. I ran to my mother's room where she was still asleep.

"Mommy, mommy wake up, there is fire in the kitchen!" She jumped up, ran to the kitchen and screamed.

"Where's your brother?!" she yelled at me.

"He's upstairs in the room," I said startled by her panic. She grabbed me with one arm and led me outside into a cold winter night.

"Go to Mr. Walker's house and tell them to call the police!"

Mr. Walker was our next-door neighbor. She went back in the house to retrieve Nash, who was still sleeping. I'm not sure what happened next but I do remember being in our neighbor's home and watching my mother on the couch, her face buried in both hands, crying. I felt helpless. I wasn't sure exactly what the fire would mean for our family or what we'd lost in the fire. But I was deeply concerned because my mother was upset and I couldn't figure out why or how I could fix it.

In the months following the fire, the house was repaired and we moved back in. It felt familiar, but it looked different. Somehow the fire had actually made the house better, and I remember going back into the kitchen where I saw the fire, and there were no signs that there'd ever been a fire. The only trace of it was in my mind.

Smallville

Smallville and I have been best friends for over twenty years. I don't remember how we became friends or why. But after my blood brothers, he is the closest person on earth to me. Our bond is carefree and uncomplicated. He's important to me because he knows all my secrets, which is both comforting and scary. Over the years, we've both changed and distance has often separated us, but we've always remained close. When we were teenagers, his grandmother spoiled him in ways that I can totally relate to. She bought him his first car when he was fifteen, a tan, two-door Chevy hatchback. She didn't care that he didn't have a license yet. "I don't want my baby on no bus! It's too dangerous out on these streets," she'd say.

She was right. The family lived in Englewood on the South Side of Chicago, a place often described as one of the most dangerous neighborhoods in America. "Now you gonna drive this car till he gets his license, and y'all be careful," she said looking at me.

"Okay," I said, and off we went. It was not a problem since we spent most of our time together anyway. We went to the same school, attended the same church, and sang in the choir together. We had no cares in the world. When we weren't together, he'd drive up and down every side street in Chicago to find me wherever I was. What would normally take fifteen minutes became a forty-five-minute excursion to my house. Our arrangement worked well until he finally got his license, then I had trouble finding him. I'd wait at home for hours for him to pick me up.

Our friendship has endured numerous challenges and weathered countless changes that life brings. Sometimes all I could do for him was lend a sympathetic ear and be there when needed. During my divorce, his empathetic critiques were invaluable as I pondered the meaning of life and my future.

His children are my children, his wife is my sister, and they're all my family. We both love Superman, though I believe he loves Superman more than I do. He has a permanent bruise on his head from an incident I still laugh at him about. When we were kids, our mothers would pin towels around our necks so we could run through the house or the back yard playing Superman. Once, taking the fearless superhero thing a bit too far, Smallville leaped from the top of the wooden steps of his mother's brownstone as if flying through the air, and fell and knocked himself unconscious. We still laugh about it to this day.

One day he said to me, "I have to go back home," his eyes brimming with tears. "I don't want to, but I don't have a choice." My friend's father was dying of terminal cancer. His mother, who was her husband's primary caregiver, had suffered much of her adult life under the dark shadow of depression. She battled the debilitating disease for more than two decades. Under the staggering weight of her husband's imminent death and her own deepening depression, she finally took her life.

Still grieving for his mother, my best friend was forced to summon the strength to be there for his father who was still holding on to life, valiantly fighting to support his son and the rest of the family. Two months after losing his mother, my best friend's father lost his noble battle against cancer.

My heart ached for my friend. Within two months, he'd suffered the unthinkable loss of both parents. I wasn't sure what to say to him other than, "I am so sorry for your loss." Words seemed such empty vessels to convey my heartfelt sorrow for my friend.

About a year later, we talked and reflected on the past months. We laughed at times. At other times, we sat quietly thinking about the words we spoke. We talked about the traumatic changes in our lives and how weird life seems sometimes. He talked about being with his dad in those last weeks and how grateful he was to have made the choice to go home and be with him. He said he asked him all the questions that the boy in him was afraid to ask but the man would not let him ignore any longer. He said they talked about the good times and the bad times that all families share, and they grew closer before he passed away.

I completely understood when he told me that talking with his father that way helped him manage his own grief. Being so close to my friend's grief made me think about my family. I realized I had lingering questions of my own

Chatham

My parents divorced when I was twenty years old, after being separated for five years. I had a great childhood filled with love and, for a time, the adoration of being the youngest child until my younger brother was born when I was ten. I had no clue of the private tensions between married couples. All I saw and felt were my parents' love for me and my older brother.

As I got older, they stopped hiding the acrimony that existed between them or I became more adept at taking my parents' emotional temperature. There were many happy times. We have family albums filled with snapshots of joyous holidays, birthdays, and other occasions when everyone seemed happy. So I know they happened. But they play in my mind like scenes from a silent movie full of facial expressions but no sound.

I still remember the lukewarm atmosphere of our home during my early teen years when it became difficult for my parents to talk to each other without arguing. I remember wishing they wouldn't talk at all because inevitably it would lead to a fight. Subconsciously, I equated silence with peace and harmony, believing that conversation ultimately leads to tension and dissent. I remember feeling conflicted during those tense times, unsure of whether to console my mother or my father. I learned that humor was always a good way to cut tension in our home, and I taught myself how to make my mother smile, hoping that laughing would ease her pain. I learned how asking my father a question about the Bible could distract him enough that he'd forget why he was upset.

My middle child status allowed me to strike an emotional balance early in my life and assume the self-appointed role of family intermediary. To do so, I had to be acutely aware of what was happening around me and sometimes overly sensitive to the emotional needs of others. Eventually, I trained myself to do that not just with my family, but with almost everyone around me.

Actually, my role had already been defined for me before I was born. My older brother is my father's namesake. Nash Shaffer III was my parents' firstborn, the cherished child favored by family and friends alike. He is naturally gifted and likable. He possesses a passionate and sensitive heart, and is uncommonly caring. Where I am a raging introvert, Nash is the consummate extrovert, always meeting people, always open to people. I have often marveled at his ability to settle into any situation and enjoy the simplest things in life.

He is shorter and a bit thicker than I am from the weight he put on in college trying out for the football team. He also has the distinguished eyes and handsome facial features of our Native American ancestors. He is earthy and loves the outdoors. He enjoys fishing, hunting, gardening, and the like. I enjoy none of those things.

"Pat, come go camping with me," he'd ask.

"The only way I'm going camping with you is if the Ritz-Carlton will let us set up a tent in the lobby," I'd reply without hesitation.

I've lived in his shadow most of my life. We're both ministers now, and truthfully he is a much better expositor of the Bible than I am and a gifted preacher.

Someone once shouted his name at me when I was about sixteen years old: "Nash!"

"No," I said quietly, glaring at him as I turned around.

"Oh, you Nash's little brother," he continued. I walked away mumbling something that was not nice.

For most of my early life outside of my home I had two names, "Nash" or "Nash's Little Brother." I felt buried under three generations of Nashes, and it frustrated me to no end. Instead of fighting what became a running insult, I turned inward.

For ten years I was the youngest member of the family. I love my father, but even as a child I knew my older brother had a bond with him that I did not. Although he loved me, I always felt there was always an invisible marker that kept us from being closer. What I did have for ten years was the unfettered and uninterrupted love and attention of a doting mother. The safest place in the world for me as a young child was my mother's lap.

When my younger brother, Christopher, was born I was forced to leave that secure place earlier than I wanted. My father and older brother were more than just father and son, they were buddies. On Sundays when my father would travel from church to church playing the organ, my brother, who is a fine drummer and a respectable pianist, would go with him hoping the church didn't have a drummer so he could play right next to him.

Even when I begged him, my father rarely took me along because he knew eventually I would start crying for my mother. And he was right. As a child, I could not be separated from her for long. I felt protected by her, and I have always been protective of her. That changed when Christopher was born on St. Patrick's Day of 1985.

Christopher is smart as one can be at 25. He has a brilliant political mind honed, as a political science major at Kent State University. His looks are exotic, which includes our mother's Seminole facial features. They are pronounced, from his thick, black eyebrows to his pointed nose and the long, thin wisps of what black folk would call "good hair."

One morning when Christopher was about eight, we were watching Oprah interview Madonna about milk baths and how healthy they are for the skin. I watched Chris quietly go to the bathroom and turn on the bathtub faucet. Through the long hallway I saw him leave the bathroom and then heard him muddling around in the kitchen. I heard the refrigerator door open and Chris searching inside it. The refrigerator closed, and I heard him walking back up the steps toward the bathroom. I watched as he turned into the bathroom carrying something concealed by his body. When I peered around the bathroom door, which was still wide open, there was Chris with a gallon of milk pouring it into his bath water.

"What are you doing?" I asked.

"Oprah and Madonna said a milk bath is good for your skin," he said.

"Yeah?" I replied.

"Yeah, so I was going to take one," he said. "We had this milk in here all the time. I could have been doing this a long time ago."

Over the years, Chris has brought me much joy with his innocence and uninhibited way of engaging life.

Second Born, Middle Son

I was about twelve years old when I began to embrace the "middle child" thing. I had to rethink my role. If my family life was a stage play, it seemed I'd become an extra. As the bond between my father and older brother solidified, and Christopher arrived receiving all the love, care, and attention newborns demand, I began to feel all alone in a house full of people. I'm well aware that my view of this is skewed. If you were to ask either of my brothers about this, they'd say that one or the other of us is the favorite.

From the moment Christopher was born, I began to redefine what it means to be me. I learned how to be alone. I learned to have meditative conversations with myself when I needed someone to talk to and no one was there but my imagination. God's garden was in my imagination and in that garden were all the things I needed to sustain myself. I began to understand my aloneness very early and how it would be a constant companion in years to come. I learned not to be afraid of being alone.

I love spacious, safe places and flourish in creative havens where ideas of love, life, and self-awareness can nourish and redeem the soul. As a teen, my room was my sanctuary. The walls were covered with pictures of all the things I love. Janet Jackson, En Vogue, the Dream Team, Jesse Jackson were all on my wall. Scores of books on wide-ranging topics filled bookshelves that lined the walls. It was full of music by Prince, Michael Jackson, Rakim and Nat King Cole. I spent hours on the floor reading *Vibe*, *Word Up* and *Ebony* magazines with my earphones on. When I wasn't listening to music, I was meditating and listening to a nature CD with rain showers and thunderstorms. I thank God for giving me parents who have always understood and embraced my strangeness.

I learned how to motivate and inspire myself, to find inspiration from observing others. I learned how to tune out harmful voices and medicate my fears and console my pain. I learned how to plot my own course toward achievement and to tell myself I could when others told me I couldn't. I learned how to be detached and distance myself from people. I've carried many of those skills into adulthood, and they've affected my relationships in both helpful and harmful ways. My relationships have suffered because I have the human desire to be with someone without knowing how to be with someone, since most of my life has been spent alone. I've listened, read, prayed, and studied many years to understand myself and the events that have helped shape my desire for love and human connection.

I'll never forget the day my mother came into my room and told me that her divorce from my father was final. Even though I was twenty, I was shocked at how deeply it affected me. On one hand, I was relieved because my parents had not been happy together for many years and a big reason they stayed together as long as they did was for my brothers and me. For that I am eternally grateful. On the other hand, I struggled with wanting to keep them together because it was familiar and comforting to me.

When she told me, I could see she'd been crying and I didn't want to exacerbate her pain, so I just listened. I knew she would be okay. But after she left my room, I lay on the bed and cried that night. No one heard me, but I wondered if I would be okay. I felt silly for being twenty and feeling that I deserved the family that lived in my head even if I'd rarely seen it in reality. I could count the handful of occasions that we had dinner or celebrated the holidays together the way I thought most families did. To this day I'm not a big holiday person and have spent most of my adult holidays alone with takeout.

As children, our parents shield us from painful truths to protect our innocence and preserve their image. As we get older, we humanize them in more real and honest ways. I am okay with the fact that there is no Santa Claus and that my parents are just people. I know beauty enveloped in strength because of my mother, Rosemary. She is my first love, and that love is a silhouette of God's unfailing and unconditional love for me. I love my mother because she is opinionated, funny, resilient, and yet tender and vulnerable.

She possesses a unique balance of wit and wisdom. I have flourished under her loving support at the same time I have felt that I could never live up to all of her expectations.

I also felt that I didn't know her story well enough. I didn't know the stepping stones of her life that led her to become the strong, independent, and funny woman I love. The open questions left holes in my consciousness. So I mustered the courage to sit and talk with her and prepared myself to ask some hard questions and hear some hard truths about her life.

First I asked simple questions about her childhood, how she met my father and their courtship. I asked when things started go bad between them and why; whether she had any regrets and what she'd do over if she could. It was a long conversation mixed with laughter and tears as she weaved together a narrative that helped me connect the dots that I'd been collecting from childhood. I learned not ask questions you don't want answers to, but still came away feeling as close to her as I could have ever been in my whole life.

My father is an only child and a prodigy. A gifted scholar of black sacred music, he's one of the last of a generation of church musicians to understand the historical subtexts of African American worship and our responsibility to our historical faith and culture. He has an encyclopedic mind and masterful memory of history and events that have shaped Gospel music and the black church as we know it. If you ask him about a concert that happened in 1967 in Chicago, he could tell you where it took place, which groups performed, what they wore that night, what time the program started, and when it ended.

Without a single music lesson, at the age of five he had perfect pitch and was able to play whatever he heard on the piano. Though it was against the law, by 12 years old, he was playing for choirs and groups on the historic Jubilee Showcase.

With all his superlative gifts, my father can be extremely stubborn and detached. Our relationship is caring and warm, but distant. His love for me is undeniable, but it has never been expressed in words. There has never been a time in my life when I asked him for something I needed and he did not do it. My questions to him were not as extensive because he is not at all comfortable talking about matters of the heart. I asked him more about things he keeps tucked away in his head. I have never had a conversation with him about how he feels, and while I've never seen him cry, I have seen him angry. I've never seen my parents embrace one another, and I've never heard them say "I love you" to one another or exchange tender expressions of affection.

Like any child, you pick up on the tension between your parents and wonder about the source of their unhappiness. "Is it me?" was the only question my young mind could come up with at the time, and I often wondered — if I wasn't there, would they have been happy and still together?

As I've grown up, I've begun to see them in ways that are just and righteous. With that has come great compassion, as I better understand the moments that shaped their early lives together. I arrived humbly at the conclusion that I've been blessed with parents that absolutely loved me and would give their lives to keep me safe. They were not perfect, but they didn't have to be because they were mine and I was theirs. My love for them has only grown over time as they invested the best of themselves in me to insure that I would be a worthwhile individual. They made a home for me and my brothers, and were committed to parenting us even when we didn't like or appreciate it. I know now more than ever that no situation is perfect, but families are made of people who do their best even when it may not be enough.

There are no limits to my parent's love for me and they've always found a way to sustain their love even when I disappoint them. That limitless love frees me to love myself, and to allow those I love to disappoint me, and for me to still love them just the same.

Part Three

CHAPTER IX

Make Love with Me?

Every question I ask is about love, every move I make is toward love.

After many hours of therapy, I began to silence voices that had misled me for years — and remember who I was. Sometimes you don't know who you are until you understand who you are not. While I'm still learning, I recognize now that I'm more than the emotional bruises left by people who said they loved me and then left me in my own self-inflicted pain.

Looking back, I understand that my self-loathing started long before I got married. In a sense, I was predisposed to hate myself, then justified it theologically in a church where guilt left me looking for love and affirmation from everyone except myself. My religion taught me about God's love, but undermined it with fear and loathing that suffocated my life and loves. My therapist helped me begin to unload the heavy, emotional baggage that was weighing me down like a beast of burden.

I remember God now, and I remember God's love for me. I remember that I'm worthy of love not because of someone else's presence in my life, but because I was created with love. While that love may be battered and bruised, it stayed with me even when I pushed it away.

During this time, my mind was reopened to ideas that shaped Christianity and the world. I spent hours in Borders reading great minds from James Baldwin to Reinhold Niebuhr and Paul Tillich. I happened upon a passage from St. Augustine's *Confessions* that still speaks to me today:

Where did I find you to make your acquaintance in the first place? You could not have been in my memory before I learned to know you. Where then could I have found you to learn of you, if not in yourself, far above me? Place has here no meaning: further away from you or toward you we may travel, but place there is none. O Truth, you hold sovereign sway over all who turn to you for counsel, and to all of them you respond at the same time, however diverse their pleas. Clear is your response, but not all hear it clearly. They all appeal to you about what they want, but do not always hear what they want to hear. Your best servant is the one who is less intent on hearing from you what accords with his own will, and more on embracing with his will what he has heard from you. Late have I loved you, Beauty so ancient and so new, late have I loved you.

Home Sweet Home

I arrived at my apartment with no indication that anything was wrong. After a long day at work, home was my retreat, and I enjoyed the solitude of living alone. I barely knew my neighbors and rarely saw them partly because of our work schedules and partly because I rarely entered through my front door. Most of the time, I came in through a back entrance closer to the garage. This time I entered the front of the building to get my mail. Heading up the stairs I saw some unusual scuff marks on the hallway wall leading to my front door.

The building was clean, but hardly luxurious. The hallways smelled of incense. And the scuffs on the wall looked strange. I followed them to my front door; which was slightly ajar. I knew I hadn't left it open. I slowly pushed on it, being careful not to touch the doorknob. I walked in, slowly peering around the door, well aware that I might encounter an intruder who was not yet finished shopping in my home. After making sure the place was empty, I surveyed the damage and took inventory of what was missing, still holding my book bag.

As I stood in my bedroom and looked around, I suddenly lifted the bag above my head and slammed it on the floor. An angry stream of cuss words gushed from my lips like Niagara Falls. After my tantrum, I called the landlord and the police. Neither was helpful, but I did appreciate the landlord's remorse.

It didn't take much searching to see that my television, all my Prince CDs (including some rare bootleg rehearsal tracks), some jeans and a couple pairs of Jordans were missing. My PlayStation 2, which doubled as a DVD player, was also gone. Though terribly inconvenient, I quickly concluded that all these things could be replaced, and I started thinking about what to do next.

That night it was extremely quiet, no television or radio. The loudest thing in the whole place was my thoughts echoing through my mind. I was angry because my things were gone. But I was even more upset that my space had been violated. Someone had invaded my home and intruded upon the peace and safety that I coveted. It was a great opportunity for a pity party, so I ordered pizza and bought ice cream at a nearby convenience store.

I have several routines before going to bed. Like clockwork, there are things that must be done before lying down. One is to place all my jewelry in a box. I only have two rings, my wedding band that I'd not stopped wearing, and a diamond ring my grandmother gave me as a wedding gift. The ring belonged to my late grandfather. The morning of the break-in I decided not to wear my grandfather's ring. As I opened the box, I noticed it wasn't there. The realization that the band was gone deepened the depression I was already struggling to overcome. Everything else that was stolen that day could be replaced by a quick trip to Target. But my grandfather's ring was one of a kind. It was a symbol of a deep connection that I shared with him and a constant reminder of where I came from. This ring had been passed down into my care. On my watch this priceless token was gone.

I never told anyone in my family about what I really lost that day. For weeks, I searched local pawnshops and anywhere else the ring might turn up. I eventually gave up, realizing I'd never find it. The ring wasn't love; it was a symbol of love given to me by my grandmother. Losing the ring has not diminished the love I hold in my heart for my grandfather. I have learned that love can be recreated.

Patrick the Chef

    Grandfather was a wonderful cook. A thin man, about five feet nine inches tall, my grandfather was already bald by the time I was a teenager. All that was left of the once thick head of smooth black hair were the thinning salt and pepper wisps around the sides and back. As his family migrated north to Chicago and settled on the city's west side, they bought a classic brownstone on Millard Avenue. Brothers and sisters pooled their resources, and eventually acquired three brownstones within a two-block radius. All of them had gardens in the back yard. There was a flower garden full of roses, daffodils, and tall sunflowers, and a vegetable garden complete with cucumbers and a variety of peppers, tomatoes, greens, and watermelons.

    When my older brother and I would visit, there were always freshly picked vegetables on the table. I was my grandfather's helper. My job was to wash them. They were then ready to be sliced at beautiful symmetric angles that fascinated me. I wasn't allowed to cut them since I was young. But he taught me about different spices, like thyme, oregano, and basil, and which ones go into what dishes and why.

    Grandfather didn't use measuring cups; he knew just how much to add, sometimes by pouring a little bit of the spice in his hand. It was a magical and special time for me. I was so proud when someone said a dish was good that I'd let out a toothless grin and shout, "I cooked it!" I don't think I ever left the kitchen when he was there.

    As I got older, I got more cooking lessons from my grandmother, my mother, and even my father. All of them helped broaden my culinary skills. When I tell people that I can cook, the response is often some condescending remark about hotdogs or whether it's food anybody can eat besides me. I smirk because what they don't know is that all my life cooking has been a creative outlet for me. A meal is a work of art. Pulling together the right ingredients is just the beginning. Knowing how to mix and blend and heat, and having the patience to allow it all to come together is what makes a good dish.

Co-Creating

I appreciate creative genius in all aspects of public and private life, and it has altered the way I perceive love and relationships. Just as we must be co-creators with God to have the life that we desire, we must partner with each other to create the loving relationships we want.

When I was a child, we had everything I believed we needed to live. We had lights and heat. There was furniture and food and all the other essentials for living. When I went to college, I assumed that blankets, sheets, and towels would come with room and board. I was surprised to learn that wasn't so. I took that same false assumption into marriage — that when we married our love would supply everything we'd need to satisfy our youthful ambitions. But much like our first apartment, love came unfurnished.

Being six foot four, I'm extremely space conscious. After much searching, I found a place that didn't make me feel like I was living in a closet. It was about the fifth apartment I'd seen. I was looking for two superficially specific things. The first was a bathroom with a mirror high enough over the sink that I didn't have to bend to see myself. The second was the kitchen cabinets. The landlords would inevitably ask what I was looking for and I'd reply, "Just checking out the cabinet space." The next day I'd call and tell them I wasn't interested because I was looking in the kitchen cabinets to see what kind of pots and pans they had.

"Mom, these places were the dumps," I complained to her about my apartment search. "They didn't even have any pots or pans in the kitchen."

"Are you serious, boy?" she replied. "Apartments don't come furnished. Whatever you want in them you have to put in there yourself."

The Love We Never Made

When my former wife and I moved into our first apartment, it was spacious but empty. It was in a well-kept older building and the apartments had been rehabbed. It smelled of new paint and moth balls. It had white walls and beige carpet throughout. The building was heated by a central furnace with radiators in each apartment.

The winter we were together there was unbearable at times. We lived on the third floor, which I didn't mind until the first time we went grocery shopping and I had to carry bags of food up three flights. Living on the third floor was also a heating disaster, because the furnace didn't work and we got no heat at all. We got a space heater for the bedroom and kept the door shut. When it was seventy-five degrees in the bedroom, it was forty degrees in the rest of the apartment. When the furnace was working, being on the third floor meant that all the heat rose to our apartment. With the moisture from the radiators, it felt like a swamp even when we opened all the windows. Many nights we took the mattress off the bed and slept on the floor because it was so much cooler.

One of the rooms had a cedar closet. Like most couples, we fought over closet space. Of course, I lost. If we had four closets in the apartment, three and a half were hers. One closet was for her shoes, another for her coats and sweaters and the other for her seasonal wear. My closet, the smallest, was for my clothing. Still the modest, two-bedroom, one-bath apartment where we began our lives together was warm because she was there.

The whole time we lived there we never really furnished the place, and I never really noticed. It was full of the possibility of lasting love. But our love, like the apartment, was never furnished with all the essentials. The care, concern, and support that make love viable were often painfully absent. Maybe my general impatience with life or my aloofness kept me from noticing that we weren't connecting in ways that could sustain us for the long haul. Love is patient, and it's like a patient in a hospital with specific needs for health and healing.

We got married, but we never made the love we needed to have a happy life. If I could go back, I'd take every ounce of energy, conversation, and resources we spent on a wedding and invest it in the love we both desired. I understand now that a beautiful wedding doesn't make a beautiful love. Millions of women long to hear the words "Will you marry me?" But this powerful question in no way carries a guarantee of love and happiness. Love is invisible and it lives through giving and sharing. I learned the hard way that a wedding does not make love — people make love. And perhaps the next time I find someone to share the rest of my life with, the question won't be: "Will you marry me?" It will be: "Will you make love with me?"

CHAPTER X

Chest Pains

*I am blessed by the reservoir of love within the human heart;
I am loved from the inside out ...*

I wish women could hear men talk about our love for them. I've never bought into the fallacy, that black men don't love black women. We do, we may not spiritualize or theologize our relationships. But when we do talk about our love for our women, we speak of how our lives touch one another in meaningful ways and how that touch changes us, challenges us and makes us better. We tend not be overly romantic or super-sensitive about love. We may not use the colorful language women do and our words sometime may sound so foreign that they might not at first hear the love hidden inside them but it is there and it is real.

When we talk about our love for women, it often starts with her curves or the color of her eyes or some other physical attribute. But then it gradually and sometimes subtly deepens to observations about her dependability, warmth, passion, and comfort. We talk about the way she may make us feel about ourselves or how she is the other part of ourselves that we never knew was missing. We talk about our frustrations, about sometimes feeling a little displaced and belittled by how independent women can be.

Some time ago I sat down with a few childhood friends. Most of them stood with me when I got married. One was getting married, so we had breakfast to congratulate him, catch up on each other's lives and get the latest news about the impending nuptials. We had done this maybe a hundred times before. But it had been a while since the last time. In fact, it had been years since we were all together in the same room. Some had moved away; some were finishing post-graduate degrees; others were working and supporting families. So this time was special.

As teens and in our early twenties, our habit was to sit and talk. We'd talk about anything and everything. Nothing was off limits. We were there to support and challenge each other, and through that we were all enhanced.

The group is as diverse as you could imagine: in age and background, we are liberal and conservative with everything from religion to politics. Sometimes the ideological divides are sharp and discussed passionately, but ultimately they've never been vicious enough to sever the ties that bound us together as young men.

Accompanying the intellectual heft that everyone brings to the table is a corresponding hubris, which in this circle of friends is not an off-putting trait. It mostly goes unnoticed, and when it is noticed it's understood, and either affirmed or generally made fun of.

The habit of sitting and talking is not unnatural, so after the pleasantries of our greetings were over the conversations began to reflect who we are now. We talked about our health — high cholesterol, hypertension, and diabetes were the first subjects up. While we averaged being in our early thirties, a couple of us were in our mid-thirties, and talk of the prostate exam came up.

We talked about our aging parents and the frustrations of being a caregiver for the ones who used to care for you. We decided that being an adult was a highly overrated experience and reminisced on our years of wonder and youth. I was amazed at how serious life had become for all of us in ways that we almost hadn't noticed. While we'd agree that, all things considered, life was good, it was also serious in ways that were heavy and burdensome, as a full life should be.

We wondered out loud about our next life choices. Some of us pondered our paths and questioned what next steps to take. Some who were single lamented the emptiness of life while simultaneously extolling the virtues of a fluidity of movement that had not been compromised by family. The husbands for the moment lamented the slowing down of life, which was showing around their waist lines.

Through the whole conversation no one ever expressed regret for the life they had with their wife, or second thoughts about the children they'd made a covenant to raise intentionally.

When they talked about their wives, it was with respect and honor. It was not without the occasional "this woman is driving me crazy," but even that was tender and without a hint of bitterness. Some talked about the challenges of having children and were concerned about the toll it was taking on the marriages, but we reminded them that procreation alone was not the primary reason they got married, that ultimately love, patience and God's grace would fill those empty spaces between them.

I glanced at one friend who seemed a little dazed by the weight of the uncertainty before him and asked him quickly, "Why'd you get married to begin with?" He said almost in a whisper, "Because I loved her." Then we all said, "That's good enough. You all will be fine!"

The power of male bonding is essential to a healthy male life. It's not about the stereotypical strip-bar hyper-sexualized images that are played out in mainstream America. It's a rich experience that has at its base an empathic nature that permeates togetherness like a mist rising from the ground at the crack of dawn. It's replenishing to be around other men who can look at you and say, "I understand."

It's replenishing for our souls to be around other men who can look at you and say, "I understand." There were no cosmopolitans over a Four Seasons brunch followed by shoe shopping. Our time was spent simply over good coffee and waffles. It was free of pretention and posturing. It was a place where the men can be boys again, and for a few moments that was perfectly fine. Then almost on cue there is a chorus of next things:

"I got to go get new brakes."

"I got to go with my wife to my mother-in-law's house and act like I like her."

"I got to get to church for a finance meeting."

"I have to take the kids shopping for a school trip" and just like that we were adults again, returning to our beloved roles of caregiver, protector, and lover. For a few minutes that day, it was really nice to be around the brothers.

I was in the minority that day as one of two guys who were single and the only one divorced. My life was still low but I was feeling better. I was noticing things that had often slipped past me, and in some way was having my own evolution. This was an important part of it.

Where Did the Time Go?

I'd been divorced for almost two years and it was one month before my thirtieth birthday. I was feeling excited and nervous, although quietly a bit panicky. I was mourning my twenties, which were all but gone now, and was asking myself, "What am I going to do with the rest of my life?" I felt so far that this life experiment, however ambitious, was failing. I'd squandered my twenties chasing after illusions. Now thirty was staring me in the face and I had the sense that I was entering a phase where I couldn't make any more excuses.

I was not a doe-eyed, naive twenty-something who had a lot of plans and expected everything to work out just the way I wanted it to. I was going to be thirty and, along with my dreams, I'd taken a beating and was a bit bruised but sobered by a world that was unrelenting in its expectations.

I'm a morning person. Rising early means you can maximize the time in your day. I need to feel like I accomplish things, so I only lay down long enough to get back up. My sleeping habits are off kilter a bit. Writing and thinking in the middle of the night is my norm. It's one of the luxuries of living alone.

Oftentimes, when I decide not to work, I can watch television or listen to an audio book while drifting to sleep. It's comforting to know that I'm not disturbing anyone. I never jump out of bed when I awake, but usually take a moment to gather my thoughts and think through what I must do first. I check my phone to read texts or listen to voicemails, turn on ESPN, then move around a bit to make sure all body parts are working before putting a foot on the ground.

One morning I reached to grab the remote control from the nightstand when I felt something odd. I woke up feeling a striking soreness in my chest with faint heart palpitations. I laid back down looking at the ceiling and listening to the television. I shrugged it off like men most often do, thinking maybe I'd slept wrong and all I needed was to stretch, go about my day, and I'd be fine.

As I entered the bathroom for the morning ritual, I took off my shirt and stared at my chest. There was bruising slightly above my left breast. It was swollen but not alarmingly so, and the color looked purplish, though only slightly. I was concerned, but again shrugged it off thinking it was some sleeping anomaly and it would go away as my day went on.

As I put my clothes that morning I was careful not to hit or disturb that spot in any way. It was sensitive to the touch and not in a good way. As I arrived at work that morning, I was conscious of the space I was in, and as I greeted people took care not to allow anyone to come too close. No one knew I was in pain and I preferred to protect myself rather than let anyone know my condition.

After a couple of hours I'd forgotten about it until a poignant reminder happened. As I sat at my desk and reached for something, I forgot for a moment that I was in pain. A sharp pain ran from my chest down through my left arm to my hand. I was shocked and felt the palpitations increase in ferocity and frequency. I was in crisis and my heart jumped inside my chest. I quickly opened my suit jacket and used my right hand to feel my chest, trying to reassure myself into calmness by my own touch.

Running my hand over my chest, I discovered that the tender lump had grown in size since the morning. I scurried to the bathroom, concerned and in pain, opened my shirt and looked in the mirror to discover that the lump was worse than I imagined. It was large and discolored in more than a pronounced way. I came to the conclusion that this wasn't something that would go away on its own. I went into the office of my boss, who also happened to be a childhood friend, and informed him of the situation. "I think I should go to the doctor."

"What's wrong?" he asked. I told him of my discovery, and then went to the doctor.

I sat anxiously in the waiting room, very out of sorts mentally and emotionally. My vocation in the pastorate usually has me on the other end of this equation. I was not conditioned to be cared for, and the attention given at the doctor's office is a bit uncomfortable. My life's work is care-giving. I was not conditioned to be cared for, and the attention gtiven at the doctor's office proved to be a bit uncomfortable. I'm the one who visits the sick and sits with members who need comfort in a situation like this. This time I was the one who was uncertain, afraid, and confused as to what I'd find out about my own health.

After the examination and an X-ray, the doctor concluded it was a mass that had to be removed very soon. "We will remove the tissue and have it biopsied to know whether it is benign or cancerous." In shock, I quietly asked, "CANCER?"

I left the doctor's office dazed and frightened, gathered my things and walked through the waiting area with my head down, looking at my feet and wondering, *What's going to happen?* Who do I tell? Can I go through this and not tell anyone? I was submerged in questions again.

I approached the lobby still gazing at the ground, purposely not looking at anyone. It had been such a long day and I was emotionally spent. Trying to hold myself together, just walking and not hearing anyone, I heard someone say, "Pat!" It was my boss and friend, and it was comforting to see him so that moment became a little less lonely for me. As we walked to my car, I was still quiet.

He asked what the doctor said and I told him. His expression didn't move. He just said, "Okay." To know him is to understand that he has "Dr. Spock" tendencies of wearing feelings and thoughts below the surface. In retrospect, he was the perfect person for me to be with at that moment. On the drive home I stopped for some ice cream and root beer — essential coping utilities for the night ahead.

Returning home that night, I immediately felt how empty the house was again, the aloneness was profound. There was another time that aloneness was profound.

Perils of a Sweet Tooth

One night I was eating a piece of cake in bed. I have a weakness for sweets as I wind down my days. While eating, I began to choke. Immediately I thought I could just drink some water, clear my throat, and I'd be okay, but it was more serious than that. My throat locked and I couldn't get my mouth open to take a sip of water. I got out of bed and struggled to straighten my body. As I did that I fell to the ground, unable to breathe. I was scared that I couldn't catch my breath and thought in that moment I was going to die.

I rolled over to try to stand up. My eyes were watering and everything seemed hazy. I thought about my family, they wouldn't know I was gone. No one had a key to my apartment. How long would it take someone to find me?

I kept struggling and ultimately freed myself of whatever was lodged in my windpipe. I sat on the ground taking deep breaths, wiping tears from my eyes and trying to calm my shaking hands. I thought about the hazards of living alone, about the hazards of being a bachelor. It was either get married or get a medic alert button, which sounded like a great idea.

My ex-wife and I had not talked at all since our divorce was finalized, which was about three years at that time. I thought of her often, more often than I wanted to. We had life plans, but after the divorce and now with the threat of cancer at 30, life seemed like it was so short. The things that drove us apart seemed so small now and life seemed terribly unfinished for me. And here I was staring mortality in the face, contemplating dying — and dying alone.

The good ones die young, I thought. I looked at myself in the mirror that night and became angry at my body that had betrayed me in some way. I understood the spirit and body in a nuanced shade of understanding. My spirit and mind were fine but my body was doing things I didn't want it to do and I was too young for this. "Why me?" I asked no one in particular that night.

Divorce left me a half-domesticated, partial husband and a wholly single 30-year-old guy living alone for the first time in his life, now sick and scared. I'd been tamed to come home after work and expect food, conversation, and duties that go along with being a husband. I was used to the routine of a marital lifestyle, but as a single man I'd kept the routine even though there was no one to come home to. I sometimes looked outside my window at night, watching people walk past or drive by, and got jealous of the fact that they were living and moving.

My life for the most part was spent waiting for morning to come again. My instincts were to call her. She was still etched in my heart. Because of that I vacillated from being profoundly sentimental to angry that I'd not been able to let go yet. In the past her voice had been comforting, for the most part at least. I loved her voice. But there was too much pain between us, too many things not said between us. I used to be her husband, and this was one of those "for worse" times when I needed her but I wasn't her responsibility anymore. Men don't heal themselves in the same place we hurt ourselves, so going back for comfort was not an option. In some ways, that desire seemed selfish of me.

Lovesick

It is an understatement to say divorce is hard, even when it's the only and most responsible decision to make. She didn't want a divorce, and truthfully neither did I. Though I loved her, I'd stopped believing that we could ever be happy together. Love sometimes means setting what you love free, even if it hurts you. As a man, we protect what we love, even if that means sometimes disappointing those we love in the process.

I wanted her to be happy. She was young, smart, and beautiful, and I knew that she'd find someone to share all the moments we talked about but never had with each other. At this point, since I was sick, in hindsight it seemed like the right thing to do. I didn't know what was about to happen with my health and wouldn't have wanted her to live the rest of her life a grieving widow. I thought I'd done her a favor.

But inaudibly and selfishly I needed her and she wasn't there. If you ever talked to either one of us about what happened and why we're not together, I'd say she left me, she'd say I pushed her away — and time has told us we're both right. I wonder about time, it's such a mystery to me. Time is unyielding to our pain and station of life.

There are few things as constant as time. It moves forward and sometimes carries us kicking and screaming along with it. It cares nothing about the breaks we need when we pause for a moment, like a runner just finishing a hundred-mile marathon. With our hands on our knees, gasping for air and trying to catch our breath, when we look up time tells us, "Keep it moving."

In its disconnection from whatever state we may find ourselves in emotionally, there is wisdom to time. As it moves us forward, it also gives us distance from our past, which can change our perspectives about our journey. Most of us never look over our shoulder to see how far we've come and to notice that every step we take moves us farther from who we once were. When I look back at my former wife and myself at twenty-two, I have great compassion and pity on them. Everything in their hearts was right and pure; they just weren't equipped to love out all the things time brought across their paths. My heart is sorrowful for every pain they had because of each other, but time has taught me that, through all of those things, God has melded and molded well the scattered pieces, which have become distinctive and beautiful.

The day of the surgery, I was nervous but you couldn't tell. My emotions were able to live underneath. I was thinking of my parents, my brothers, and my grandmother. I was just so uncertain of what was going to happen. If I had my choice and had to die, I'd choose to die on the operating table instead of after a prolonged bout with cancer. I've grown accustomed to short, meaningful goodbyes instead of days and nights of impending sickness and death.

My older brother drove me to the hospital and we met my parents and grandmother there. They assigned me a room, told me to take off my things, and put on a gown. It was cold in the hospital so I asked for a warming blanket. My parents, grandmother and older brother joined me in the room. We sat and talked for a minute and then became quiet.

My grandmother asked if she could look at my chest. I pulled back the gown from my shoulder. She cringed and put her head down. By this time the lump was extremely discolored and swollen. I took a moment to tell them how much they meant to me and apologized for being sick and for not knowing what was going to happen. I said goodbye to my parents while successfully holding back tears. Like a little boy, I was so scared. I didn't want to leave them and didn't want them to leave me. I kissed my parents. My brother tried to lighten the mood and asked if this was my way of getting breast implants. I responded by leaning on the sign language courses I'd taken in college and gave a quick gesture out of the view of my parents.

As they wheeled me into the operating room, I heard the wheels of the gurney creaking with the corresponding echo that came from a long empty hallway. It was quiet and dense. I didn't know what was going to happen. I thought that if I pass away, I have no children. Nothing lasting to carry on in my absence, I'll be nothing but a memory in the minds of family and friends that in time will fade away. Regret was washing across my mind. I lay on the operating table, knowing I had hidden what I felt from those around me. I felt guilty, thinking, *did I say goodbye to everyone I should have? Do they know I love them? Will I ever see them again?*

I quickly guessed that in my own way I was caring for them. For them to know what was going on inside me would have no doubt added to their anxiety, so I internalized the idea that I was in some way grieving my own death. Like Tupac, Biggie, Kurt Cobain, I would die young and full of promise. The only difference is, I'd die with less money, talent, and notoriety. I thought, *this really kicks rocks right now!*

Before the anesthetist put me under, I remember looking at the clock on the wall to my right. It was moving as clocks do. I thought that my time was in God's hands and felt peaceful. As my eyes closed, I drifted to a place I cannot remember, but my last conscious thought was: Would I ever get a chance to live again? Will I ever get a chance to love again?

Recovering Love

The surgery went well. I woke up in a brightly lit room with a big-bosomed Mexican woman standing over me. She was an English speaking woman with a heavy accent, she spoke and I recognized my name. As I slowly opened my eyes, the light was bright and everything was hazy. I saw her beautiful face standing over me with a white light shining behind her head, and thought, *I must be dead. I must be in heaven, apparently in the Los Angeles section, which means that all my time on earth I've been Mexican and didn't know it.*

Realizing this was not heaven but indeed the South Side of Chicago, I was relieved. Still feeling the effects of the anesthetic, I was aware of my surroundings. My mother met me in the recovery room with my older brother. After a few minutes of sitting up I wanted to put on my clothes — I was freezing. After dressing I sat for a few moments. I was hungry, not having eaten since the previous night. They brought me a ham sandwich and some orange juice. It was delicious only because I was hungry.

I was taken home. My apartment was on the third floor but I don't remember how I got up the steps. I sat on my bed, while my brother and mother grabbed my medicine and other things from the car. All of a sudden, I felt sick. I got that swollen glands and watery mouth feeling and knew what was about to happen.

I tried calling for someone but didn't have the strength to yell. My bathroom was on the other side of the apartment. I was about to vomit but had to make it to the bathroom. The carpet cleaned just before I went into the hospital. I climbed out of bed but was dizzy and too weak to stand. With one hand over my mouth I crawled to the bathroom. Reaching the bathroom threshold I could no longer hold it and vomited on the floor.

I was sweating, still queasy with one hand on the floor and the other on the commode when my brother found me. He helped me stand up and then sat me down on the corner of the tub. He washed my face and gave me something to rinse my mouth with. "It's okay; it's just the result of the anesthetic being in your system. You will be fine." I looked up and said to him, "Oh, I was going to sue the hospital for that ham sandwich they gave me. Thank you, Nash."

After an hour or so, I told my mother and brother to go home. I was feeling okay and it had been a long day for everybody. They reluctantly agreed. I slept a deep sleep that night, then woke up and went to the bathroom. My chest did not hurt per se but felt extremely heavy. I looked in the mirror and saw that my chest was heavily bandaged, with a slight sign of blood that could be seen coming from the wound. I looked at myself and thought that I looked like one of those guys in the movies that had gotten shot in the shoulder. *Cool.*

My recovery was spent indoors for the next three weeks. Slowly but surely I was getting my strength back. I spent a lot of time thinking. I felt like I had another chance and that I didn't know how long I had left. I was getting ready to be thirty. Now what was I going to do? The experience changed me forever. I got more serious about life. I didn't know who I was but sometimes you learn who you are by discovering who you are not. I was not who I'd become, I was not who some people wanted me to be, I wasn't who my religion had made me to be. I felt free to give myself permission to come into a deeper understanding of purpose and personhood. I felt like I'd been given the gift to fly since I was a child but had never used my wings before. I spent time letting my imagination give me sounds, swirl colors, shapes, fonts, textures in my mind of what kind of life I could have if I wanted it. I communed with God and angels made from the creative force that was in the beginning. My heart was let loose like a child in an open field. My night dreams never ended and my daydreams were orgasmic. I was being born again, which is the first step to love. What I saw in my head I knew I could have by the mere fact that it was there. It was my signal that allowed me to conceive of possibilities.

I went for the follow-up with my doctor when he called and said he had the results of the biopsy. My older brother drove me. We sat in the doctor's office. When he entered he asked me the standard questions about pain, how I was sleeping, and the like. He asked me to take off my shirt. As he took the dressing from the wound, I noticed a small cotton ball about the size of a pencil eraser protruding from my chest. He looked circumspectly at it and pulled it quickly. My initial shock was that he seemed brusque with the area that for me was still tender and I was psychologically still protective of.

When he grabbed the tip of the cotton ball and yanked it from my chest, I was in shock as he pulled about fourteen inches of cotton from my chest that — I discovered in that moment — was tucked there to soak up whatever bleeding would occur. With my mouth agape, I was stunned. It was the most horrendous pain I'd ever experienced. It felt as if someone set a fire inside my chest. It took a minute to compose myself. After regaining my bearings, the doctor informed me that the tissue biopsied was benign and that I'd be fine.

"Doc, why did this happen?"

"We aren't sure."

"Will it happen again?"

"We're not sure."

I felt my eyebrows frown in frustration. I couldn't understand how this could happen to me and I had no answers. I walked to the car with a mixture of emotions but did not lose sight of the fact that what I'd been through had just served to open my heart to hope itself, and that little seed of knowing was the cornerstone for the life I wanted. And it all started with a little chest pain.

CHAPTER XI

Reflections in Love

I loved and I lost sight of me; I couldn't see love looking back at me.

Right after my thirtieth birthday, while recovering from surgery to remove the growth from my left breast, I spent a lot of time pondering my mortality and uncertain future. My twenties were gone, and I was getting serious about life. The only problem was I didn't know who I was. At that time, I was a mishmash of impressions pinned to me like labels by people I admired and from whom I sought affirmation.

Sometimes you don't know who you are until you know who you are not.

The path to self-discovery begins with shedding false and misleading characterizations imposed upon you. Before you can accurately define who you are, you must undefine who you are not. It left me momentarily impotent to move forward with life. At thirty, I didn't know what I wanted because I didn't know who Patrick was. I woke up each morning desperately longing to know who I was and what God wanted me to do with the rest of my life.

A friend in Dallas says I'm a better athlete than basketball player. I disagree. After the surgery scare, my physical health became much more important, so I joined a gym. It's one of those franchise health clubs for busy, working people, and what attracted me first was that it was open 24 hours a day. Touring the facilities, I found the flat-screen televisions, smoothie bar, and exercise equipment very appealing. The gym offered free yoga and Pilates classes, along with intensive instruction in body sculpting and muscle building. But I really joined because of the basketball court.

As a teenager, the basketball court was a place of great joy. I've loved the game as long as I can remember. I played in high school and on intramural teams in college. I love the competition and the communion of team sports. But also I remember going to the basketball courts around my home when I had a lot on my mind. It was where I could be alone with my thoughts, a place to reflect, pray, and think through problems, and allow my spirit to exhale. I always came away from the court feeling lighter and unburdened.

I don't remember how often I actually played during my twenties, but I was excited about getting back on the court regularly because playing would provide cardiovascular activity while working on my game with some new competition. My only concern — I knew my legs were gone. I knew I'd probably never jump as high or run as fast as I once could. But basketball ultimately is about putting the ball in the hoop and I still knew how to do that. I've been blessed with a nice jump shot and was returning to the court as a wily veteran. I said to myself, *In three months, I'll be back to my old game.*

At first I began to shoot around by myself. The gym was usually empty so it was perfect. Basketball is a muscle memory sport, and the movements of my feet and the trajectory of my shot slowly started coming back. It felt good, and I began thinking and praying on the court as I had when I was a teenager.

After about a week, I began to play with other guys at the gym. It's always funny how these pickup games begin. No one knows anybody or who can or cannot play. So we chose teams and started to play. I hadn't played full court basketball in over five years. When the game was over, I leaned against the wall, quietly gasping for breath, acutely aware of how every organ in my body was working overtime to keep me from passing out. I'd failed to hydrate myself, and could feel my kidneys throbbing and lungs contracting and expanding. It felt like my pancreas and even my prostate were in crisis. My muscles burned like they hadn't in years.

I'd walked into the gym with no thought of my body. I walked out painfully aware of each excruciating step. Each time I lifted and lowered my leg it was a major event. My pride was all that hurried me forward. I couldn't let the guys see me struggling. I finally found a brief respite on a nearby bench. Gingerly lowering myself, I felt the full weight of my body sink into the bench cushion. For a long time my muscles hurt to even look at them, so I closed my eyes to conjure the strength to stand up. After a few minutes my muscles cooled down and my heart stopped racing, but I still wasn't sure I could make it up the stairs to my car.

"You okay?" the fitness coach asked as she walked by.

"Yeah, I'm good," I said, lifting my head sharply and responding in as deep a masculine voice as I could muster. As she left, I hung my head again and wondered if I'd make it out of the gym.

I don't remember how I got to the car that day. As I walked through the door of the apartment, I dropped the gym bag on the floor and pushed myself along the wall to the bedroom. I sat there on the chaise, wondering if I could untie my shoes. I thought about it for a long time before doing it. After showering, I laid down for the night. I'm not a restless sleeper, but that night I lay on my back without moving a muscle. I woke up to bright, morning sunlight and the whirling ceiling fan that had been spinning all night.

I didn't move. I was afraid of the pain my first move would bring. Finally I sucked it up and made my way to the bathroom for morning ablutions. As I peered in the mirror, I saw a gray hair in my beard and a couple more on the side of my head. I would've fainted but knew I wouldn't have been able to get up off the floor. I was devastated, but determined to fight time and what was happening to my body. I gathered my things and went back to the gym. I knew I'd have to work through the pain, and that the more I engaged my body the more accustomed it would become to this renewed activity. But after a few weeks, I wasn't getting any better. In some ways, the pain was actually getting worse. The initial soreness had turned into painful creaks and pinches in my back, shoulders, and legs.

Somehow, I'd failed to notice how much younger my new basketball buddies were.

"What's going on?" I asked the six-foot-five, 215-pound beast I was about to play.

"Nothing much. You?" he replied staring at me.
"I'm good. Hey, how old are you?"
"I'll be eighteen in two weeks."
"Oh, okay," I said plainly.

I looked over my shoulder at a five-eleven, 160-pound guy doing some kind of dribbling exercise with two basketballs.

"How old are you?" I asked.

"I'm 17 too, but I just had a birthday," he said in a high-pitched voice.

This seemed odd until I walked into the middle of the court and asked everyone over 21 to raise his hand, and no one did. Turns out I'd been working out with a bunch of high school kids for over a month. I'd almost crippled myself because I hadn't looked them in the face and noticed their youth and I hadn't looked myself in the face to see that I wasn't a kid anymore.

I'd avoided looking in the mirror because I didn't really want to see myself. I was afraid to see that I wasn't twenty-two anymore. I was afraid to see that time had changed me in ways that I had yet to discern or accept, and spent a lot of time blaming myself for everything that happened to me. Though some things were my fault, some weren't. But I carried the burden of them all. To look at who I'd become would've made me accountable for who I was. Instead, I closed my eyes to the truth of the white elephant in the room just as I did on the basketball court playing with kids barely more than half my age.

If Love Was That Easy

I remember going to a friend's birthday party at a local YMCA when I was six. It was a pool party, and I was very excited. I've always loved the water and all kinds of water sports. My brother went out ahead of me while I closed our locker. As I headed toward the pool, I could hear the kids splashing around in the beautiful blue water. I ran toward the water, got to the edge of the pool and jumped as high as I could. I gathered my knees to my chest and cannonball into the water about three and a half feet from the side of the pool.

I was a good swimmer because my brother and I had lessons when we were still toddlers. Kids were playing at the other end of the pool, and the parents were seated above the pool behind a glass window, nervously mingling while keeping a watchful eye on their children. So no one saw that I'd jumped into the deep end instead of the shallow water, where all the other kids were.

As the full weight of my frame hit the water, I could still hear the kids playing. But no one was near me. I was all alone underwater trying to find the bottom of the pool so I could thrust myself upward and get some air. As I sank lower and lower unable to find the bottom, fear gripped me and I swallowed a mouthful of water. I looked up and could see the lights above the pool. I thrust my arms out to the side as if they were wings to lift myself up. When my head finally broke through the surface, I saw some of the other mothers trying to comfort my panicked mother beating against the glass as she watched her youngest son drowning.

I was still fighting to stay afloat, but my little arms were too tired, I went under again. I opened my eyes and saw the lines at the bottom of the pool coming closer and closer. Suddenly, a hand reached down, grabbed my arm and lifted me straight out of the water. The hand brought me to the side of the pool and I sat there gathering myself. My arms hurt, and I was tired. My mother made sure I was okay and then scolded me.

"Do you want to go home?" she asked.

As I thought about it, I heard the other kids having fun and decided to stay.

"No, I'm fine, Mommy. I want to go play." I walked to the end of the pool where they were playing and jumped back in. I was too young to know that I should've been scared. To me, what had just happened at the deep end had nothing to do with what was going on at the other end. There was too much fun to be had and too much cake to be eaten to let almost dying stop me from enjoying the rest of my day.

That was nearly thirty years ago. I wish loving someone again was that easy. But it's not. Maybe the best pieces of our lives are the ones grace allows us to live past and give away.

Silent Killer

Strangely in the pastorate, I have the pleasure of meeting a lot of people with different stories, lives, histories, and loves. There are common strands in the whole gamut of human experiences that bind all people together. The church is where they all converge and through process are sorted out — not by preaching and teaching alone but by connecting through community. The greatest stimulus to my own healing came as I peered into the lives of others, unbeknownst to them and even myself. Through community we were all being healed.

One couple in particular gave me some of the pieces I was missing to put myself back together again. I was supposed to be caring for them but their love helped me heal. One day I had the privilege of meeting a man named Edward Mitchell. Everyone called him "Killer." I never asked why, but deduced that you don't ask someone why others call him Killer and you don't ask the people around him why they call him Killer. Some questions are better left unasked.

Killer and I never had a conversation. When I met him, through his wife, he was in the last stages of a courageous fight against cancer — very ill, unconscious, and bedridden in a hospital. As I looked at his weak, gaunt frame, I could tell that he stood about five foot seven. On his best day he was maybe one hundred and fifty pounds. I looked at his face; his skin was almond and his eyebrows had grayish wisps throughout. With his strong chin and pronounced nose, I could tell that in his youth he was comely and as a man he was handsome.

Those qualities were still evident but because of the illness that had captured his body you'd have to study his frame to see that they were faded but there. His wife Sandra was curvaceous and full-formed, her hair was cut short, and her nails were manicured with a color I'd call beige. They were tastefully done, and by looking at her hands and the smile on her face, I knew why Killer married her. Her voice filled whatever room she was in. She was not boisterous but her presence was inviting. In my own way I understood how comforting a spirit she was as they held hands throughout their life together.

Sandra absolutely adored him. It was through her memories that I began to draw close to Killer. Her vision of herself was intertwined with his love in ways that almost seemed unreal. I heard in her voice things we all wish to hear from someone who loves us. I was listening — not just to her voice but the cadence and tone in which she described the magnanimous life that was theirs alone. Her words were placed in the air and were so full of care and tenderness that they never touched the ground. Her words created an atmosphere that enveloped me in their passion and fullness.

As we spent hours sitting beside his bed, Killer was unaware that we were even there. She began to tell me about their teenage courtship, living in rural Mississippi through the Jim Crow years, coming North to get jobs, settle, and raise a family. Sandra told me of family trips, struggles with their children, burying their own parents, and now their empty nest. She told me of times of great struggle, financially and relationally. She told me of moments when their marriage was challenged in ways that test the heart of commitment and in ways that take a piece of the soul away, and yet they remained by each other's side.

She told me of the trips around the world they'd planned to take before Killer got sick, and now she was pondering what it would be like to live without him. She pondered listless days without the man she loved, and who would she be and where would she go? I began to hear his voice through hers, a voice I imagined as boisterous, deep, and strong, yet tender and loving. I listened to her and heard how clear his laugh was and how full his love for his wife remained.

As Sandra spoke of her love for him, he lay in quiet repose. It felt as though my mind could hear him speak of the love he had for this beautiful woman. She spoke of her love for him but I knew he loved her so much more. Their love had led them to this hospital room, where she never left his side.

Hospitals are interesting places. All roads lead to the hospital. We are born there. When we're sick with fever, we're healed there. The hospital seems a selfish place. All the most dramatic and passionate moments in life somehow generally end up within its walls. I wonder if hospitals have memories. Do they capture certain moments of our lives that allow them to be compassionate for the next baby being born, the next person with complications from lupus, or the family who pulls the plug on a loved one when the quietness of death has released the spirit from the body and all that's left is a heart that didn't know it wasn't supposed to still be beating?

I imagined when they married that they didn't have this scenario in mind. When you marry someone, maybe in the back of your mind you try to imagine what "for better and for worse" means, but we never really fully do. Yet, they were here and she was doing the best she could to cope with the realities of her love and life. Her love for him was so strong; I could feel it. If love alone was the cure for his sickness, she had enough to make him healthy again. Yet in this moment, her love for him was not the answer to the difficult questions being asked of them both.

One particular day, I stopped by the hospital and came to his room to see it filled with a lot of the things he loved: pictures of his children and grandchildren; him on a boat fishing with friends; he and Sandra on a cruise in Bermuda shorts and sunglasses. On the wall, there was a handwritten banner that said, "Happy 50th Anniversary Edward and Sandra." They celebrated their 50th wedding anniversary while Killer was in the hospital, hooked up to machines, because it was important to her to celebrate their love for each other even if she had to do it alone. It was touching to witness.

A few days later Killer passed away. His memorial was like a mayor's funeral. During the wake they played all his favorite music. One band in particular that was played was his favorite: Earth, Wind and Fire. People mingled and talked, laughed and wiped away tears, but generally it was an uplifting event. I drove to the cemetery in the procession and watched a brave woman give way to her grief and anger as she yelled to the hole that held his casket, "Why did you leave me? I love you, Killer. What am I going to do now?"

Their love made me jealous. I wanted what they had but couldn't imagine having it and losing it again. Grief is the price you pay for loving someone. If you never want to say goodbye to someone, never say hello. What I didn't notice was that, in some way, my desire for love began to come back. Not the desire to be loved but the need I'd never lost, the need to love someone. I'd always thought that their kind of love story only happened in movies like the *Notebook,* but their love was real and vivid.

I just wasn't convinced that I could have my own love story again. But by watching with my eyes and listening with my heart, their love taught me that if I was to have any shot at receiving love in my life, it was going to start with me loving myself, the most challenging choice of all. I was first going to have to look in the mirror and see in my own heart a reflection of love precious enough to share with someone else.

Thank You, Frasier

After a long road trip, I was at home sitting on the floor feeling sorry for myself, channel surfing. One night I heard God speak to me in a very odd way, and it helped me begin to put my life back together again.

I have a few hobbies. I generally enjoy things that most people would find boring, like listening to rain fall on a hot summer day, or watching people walk by me as I sit in a mall. Mostly, I love solitude at home and just being alone with my own thoughts. The God I know and love communicates with us, sometimes in sundry and strange ways. God's voice is profound and life changing. I've always loved satirical comedy, and enjoy television sitcoms. But I like smart comedies. I've never been a fan of slapstick humor. I enjoy comedy only when the comedy serves some redemptive relational, social, or political value.

That's why I enjoy the television series *Frasier* starring Kelsey Grammer. One day I stopped on the show. I'd never seen it before but was familiar with the Frasier character from *Cheers*. I discovered later that what I was actually watching was the pilot episode of the show called *The Good Son*. In it Frasier is working at his call-in radio talk show when a woman calls crying and distraught over the recent break-up of a long-term relationship.

"The pain won't go away," she says to Frasier through her sobbing, weak voice. "It's like I'm in mourning or something." As she spoke, I listened and heard myself in her trembling, vulnerable voice. I didn't see her tears, but I heard her pain. She went on to say that she'd not been able to get over the break-up and move past it for some time. Kelsey Grammer has one of the most caring and warm voices I've ever heard. When he spoke to the woman as Frasier, I heard God in his voice, and the words he spoke to her touched me deeply.

"You are not mourning the loss of the person," he said to her tenderly. "You are mourning the loss of what you thought your life would be like." He paused and said, "Let it go. Sometimes things don't work out the way we want them to, but that's not always a bad thing."

Upon hearing that statement, I burst into tears, as God's voice broke through my pain and the pain began to melt away. Laying face down on the floor in my bedroom, God allowed me to pinpoint my pain. I'd been quietly depressed for months and could not understand why. On the outside, I was business as usual but on the inside, I was lost. It wasn't that I was still sad that Denae and I weren't together. It was more that I was mourning the loss of my dreams that left with her. I was mourning the part of myself that she took with her.

Like we all do in our serious relationships and marriages, we dream of life and love together. When relationships end, we're left alone with empty hopes and incomplete dreams. Our hearts succumb to emotional paralysis and we can't move past our pain — we're stuck. We don't know whether to let the dream become our life's nightmare, or wake up, recast our dreams, and redefine ourselves. By the time Denae and I got divorced, I thought we surely would've had the house and two cars with a couple of kids and a third child in the works while living and enjoying life. That had been my dream. The reality was that life had happened to me in what I thought were cruel and unfair ways, and instead I had none of what I wanted.

We see life within the context of what we want. When we engage others in a personal way through relationships, we ascribe to them a certain value and worth, and we see them as a conduit through which our vision may come to pass. When a person to whom we've ascribed such worth leaves, it can create an indescribably painful void. But watching television that night, I finally lifted my head and my heart from a very low and lonely place. Thank you, Frasier.

CHAPTER XII

Love Again

Though beautifully damaged we are, love calls. Though fainthearted we are, love calls, and we must answer again. What shall we say of love? What shall we say to love?

Sometimes my life seems like an endless series of meetings. One day, as I was leaving a speaking engagement, a young man told me he was familiar with my work and wanted to visit the church one Sunday morning. I told him he could come anytime.

"I know the ushers. I can get you a good seat," I said. We both laughed. His name was Greg, and he was a recent college graduate with a degree in business. He told me about his work supporting the senior leaders at his church. A wiry, athletic twenty-one-year-old, about six foot two and a 160 pounds, he seemed bright and energetic. He was carrying a backpack and a hand full of conference materials.

I asked if he played ball. He said he played basketball in high school and college but had torn the anterior cruciate ligament (ACL) in the last year and was in rehabilitation. "Not one hundred percent, but almost," he said. I asked if he was any good. "I got game," he replied. "When I get better, we can go to the gym and shoot."

"How old are you again?" I asked.

"Twenty-one," he said.

"Yeah, you're way too young for me to be playing, but since you most likely will be on one leg, I like my chances." We both laughed. I gathered my things, and Greg waited patiently as I exchanged pleasantries with the other conference participants. My energy and attention span was waning, but I love the small talk so I didn't mind. I sat down and continued talking with a charming group of students who had driven from Ohio to attend the meeting.

"I'd really like to talk to you about ministry," Greg said when we were alone again. "I need some direction, and I believe you should help me." His sincerity was refreshing, but I was a little apprehensive.

"Greg, it's not my custom to give ear to members of another congregation, but we can sit and talk if you just want to bounce some ideas around," I said. "Call my office next week, and we can find some time," I said, while grabbing my bag and checking phone messages.

"Thanks Pastor Patrick, I will definitely do that then," Greg said as we walked toward the exit.

The following week Greg called, and we arranged a time to meet. City of Faith is nestled in the historic South Side Chicago community of Hyde Park. It's rich not only in history, but a diverse, cosmopolitan mix of academic, civic, and social cultures. There's also a wide array of shops, boutiques, chain stores, restaurants, and cafés where people move in unspoken syncopation while working, eating, listening to music, or just watching each other. A Borders bookstore off Lake Park Avenue is the unofficial hub for all sorts of activities, from book clubs and study groups to chess games and light lunches. Greg and I decided to meet there one hot summer afternoon.

I arrived early because I hate to be late and because I love browsing through magazines and books. I picked a couple of books and found a table near the window that was unoccupied. I was immersed in one of the books when I looked up to see Greg sitting across from me. I was a bit annoyed, not because he was late, but because the book was intriguing and I wished I had more time to read. I asked him how his day was, shifting glances between his face and the book.

"Excuse me, I'll be right back," I said, hurrying down the stairs with the book. I returned it where I found it, tilting it slightly on its side as a marker so that I could find it again when I returned. I stopped by the food court and bought biscotti and a cup of green tea. I returned to the table to find Greg on the phone. As I took my seat, he motioned that he'd be a minute.

"Okay, Sweetheart, I'll call you when I leave here," he said into the phone and hung up.

"That was my fiancée," he said with a pleased look on his face. "We met when we were eighteen at my parent's church. She's in medical school now."

I could see that he was happy.

"When is the wedding?"

"In six months."

"Well, tell me about her," I said, sipping my tea while watching his face. It wasn't his words alone that caught my attention. His love and fondness for her resonated with every word he spoke as if his heart were wrapped around each one. As the words left his mouth, they seemed to dance in the air. And the weight of his words was supported by the sheer strength of his optimism for their future together. He seemed completely oblivious to any possibility that their love could fail.

"She understands me and my calling," he said. "I'm going to pastor one day, and she'll make a good first lady. We pray together, and we believe that God will bless us to be what the Word says we're supposed to be. We minister together with the youth at our church, and she's good with children.

"She doesn't want to leave her church," he added, "but she said she'd follow me as I do God's work and be my helpmate. We talked about children, but not right now. By the time I'm twenty-four, we're going to have our first child. I'm working at the gym while I'm still in school, and she works with battered women. So, we're going to save up and buy a house in two years. I just know together we can be a blessing to each other, and God will get all the glory," he said finally.

We talked for about two hours that day. I tried to be as reassuring as I could, but also offered a few thoughts to consider. We talked about his education and how I thought it was important for him to finish his program before having children and taking on the weightier responsibilities of married life. I urged him to be patient with her and himself.

"You are both young, and you can make it together," I said. "But sometimes it's going to feel like you're a failure because you don't understand each other. If you can resist the temptation to pull away from each other, you'll find reasons and ways to work things out. You should look into clinical couple's therapy before the wedding and for at least a year after the wedding. I know your church has a premarital track for you, but sometimes you need more trained eyes to evaluate your relationship and help you get a better perspective on your problems."

I asked if his fiancée had brothers and sisters.

"No, she's an only child, a daddy's girl." He sighed slightly.

"Wow, good luck with that!" I replied, laughing out loud.

We talked about living under the shadow of an ever-present father in her life and how spoiled she could be. We talked about how some realities won't change but that with patience understanding they could be managed.

When we finished, I sat staring at him silently. I hadn't noticed that by the end of our conversation both of my hands were gripped tightly around the mug I was holding. It was still half full and warm. My eyebrows were raised and tightened across my forehead. Greg seemed a little confused, as I struggled to get the words out.

He had said nothing to offend me. His words were sincere and thoughtful about his life plans and how he understood God's plan for him. But as he spoke, a faint disquiet swept through me. I felt anxious and didn't understand why.

"Well, seems like you have it all figured out," I said. "I'm sure it will all come together for you. I'm happy for you and your bride-to-be. Keep me posted on how things turn out. And if I can help in any way, let me know."

I got up rather abruptly, said goodbye and left the bookstore. As can often happen in Chicago, the bright, sunny day was now consumed by storm clouds. Leaving the bookstore, I headed east toward Lake Michigan. Walking past Harold Washington Park, I crossed a bridge over Lake Shore Drive to the lakefront. Standing on some rocks at the edge of the lake, I could see Chicago's magnificent downtown skyline and dark, smoky clouds hovering above the giant Ferris wheel at Navy Pier. Directly in front of me as I looked out upon the lake, I could see the distant flash of lightning bolts, both frightening and beautiful at the same time.

I suddenly noticed how heavily I was breathing and that I was sweating. Both my hands were clenched into fists. It took me a minute to realize that I'd run to the lake and that my face was wet not just from sweat, but from my own tears. I was dazed and at first a little disoriented. I had no clue why the conversation with Greg had triggered such emotion in me. I stood there reflecting on our exchange. There wasn't anything new, surprising, or especially profound about it. I'd heard it all before. It was just a young man sharing his dreams about life, love, and God's work.

It started to rain. Not a downpour, but the kind of delayed drizzle that drips on your face at annoying intervals. Slowly, the rain fell more heavily and the city darkened. I stood alone gazing at the monstrous, swirling clouds above my head as the angry sky poured down upon me. I didn't move. I was transfixed on solving the puzzle in my head. Like a knot in a shoelace, I had to untie it or it would unravel me. I began to talk to God out loud, and the more I talked the more it rained. I found myself apologizing for everything I'd done in my life.

I closed my eyes and lifted my head skyward. The rain washed away my tears, and I felt free. Finally, I understood. When Greg spoke, I heard myself, a gifted young man with faith, hope, and love. He had everything he needed to make the full, happy life he wanted with the woman he loved. But I couldn't be happy for him. I mourned for him, I was mourning for myself.

His life plan allowed him no room to even contemplate failure, and I knew what that felt like. When I was his age I thought that by the mere force of my will and God's grace, everything in my life, including love, would be right and simply fall into place. When I think about myself at Greg's age, I have mixed emotions. I am angry about the choices I made and in the same moment full of self-pity.

Listening to Greg forced me to hear myself and not to hate where I find myself today. Talking with Greg that day was me trying to give myself the talk that no one gave me. I was trying to give him a heads-up without sounding like an old guy who'd forgotten what it feels like to be young and in love. I talked to him about my mistakes — the times I went wrong and should've made a right instead of a left. I talked with him fully understanding a young man's wanderlust and the impatience of youth. Our conversation that day helped me to reconcile my past and be at peace with myself.

Parental Emptiness

The text message came as I sat having dinner with my mother. When I read it, I was overcome by sadness and anger. I didn't know how to respond. "I had the baby this morning at about 5 AM. It's a boy." The message was from a high school friend named Tina. She and I had been friends for more than fifteen years, keeping in touch off and on during that time. About nine months before the text, she called me and told me she was pregnant and that she and the child's father were not in love and that he'd decided not to be part of the child's life.

"I'm fine with it," she said. "I can raise my child on my own. My family supports me."

I spared her my lecture about contraceptives and offered my support as well.

"Let me know if there's anything I can do."

"I know this is a lot to ask, but do you think you might go with me to my birthing classes and help me when I deliver?"

I'd been thinking more along the lines of putting together a crib or money for baby clothes.

"It's not out of the question," I replied. "We have some time. Let's talk more about it." But after we hung up, I kept asking myself, "Do I really want to do this?"

I was approaching my mid-thirties. I had yet to have a relationship that lasted more than a year. I had no children. I could not deny my parental yearnings. I often fantasized about family life and how it would change me for the better. Children are the life of a man's legacy. If I died today, I would leave no living footprint in the earth that I was here.

I had no illusions that helping Tina would not somehow substitute for what I lacked in my life. But I was curious about the feelings I might experience in the process. So, I told her that I'd help. I was a bit nervous and excited about the birthing classes. I thought that not being the child's father would provide some safe emotional distance. I treated it all like some kind of science project. If I could develop feelings for Tina and her child, maybe it would help me if and when I had my own wife and baby.

Looking around the room, I immediately noticed that the women were attentive and engaged, and the men were trying their best not to show what I suspected: that none of them wanted to be there. I could see in their faces that I was probably the only one who actually volunteered. The classes were on Thursday night, and while that meant missing *Grey's Anatomy*, I considered being there with Tina a worthy sacrifice.

The class was fascinating and informative in an almost adolescent way for me. My only previous experience with childbirth had been a television special on PBS. My remote got stuck as they showed a woman actually delivering her baby. For junior and senior high school, I attended a private Christian institution which did not believe in sex education. So I'd missed all the up close and theoretical information about female anatomy that I was getting in Tina's class.

The nurse was warm and considerate, and encouraged us to ask questions. As the class progressed, the nurse showcased her extensive knowledge of the subject and an impressive command of the terminology associated with it. I was able to follow most of it, I was learning and it was a great experience. The instructor graciously answered all my questions, and then Tina and I moved on learning how to breathe together.

Before and after the classes, Tina and I talked about preparing for the delivery and all the other details leading up to the big event. I'd call and check to see how she was doing and if she needed anything. Such caring soon began to feel natural and nurturing for me.

What I didn't know was that several weeks before the delivery, the baby's daddy decided he wanted to patch things with Tina and try to be a father to his child.

"Ken and I decided a couple of months ago to try to make it work, so when I went into labor I called him," Tina explained in the second part of the surprise text message about the birth of her baby.

I understood. But I was disappointed, hurt, and angry that for months I was out of the picture and didn't even know it. I also hated the unseemly way she chose to tell me. I forgave her, but again, the sadness was all too familiar to me.

The Old Me?

I believe in the old adage that "our lives should be full of committed passions." My path in life has allowed me to invest my time and energy in things I care about. To that end, I support causes that are near to my heart. I met Jonathan Penworthy at a recent fundraiser for Sickle-Cell Anemia. A much-decorated war veteran and retired general in the United States Air Force, he was between seventy and seventy-five years old when we were introduced by a mutual friend.

When we got the opportunity to sit and talk at the fundraiser, I talked to him about his life, which he described as quiet and esthetically spacious for a single, older man. He'd been divorced for over twenty years and never remarried. I sat transfixed, watching him and listening to him talk about his career and the life he now leads. At one point it seemed that he wanted me to go away, but I kept asking questions because I wasn't sure I'd get another chance.

I asked him what it's like to get old, never thinking that my question could be offensive. But he was patient and very honest as he talked about the gradualness of time and how sneaky and unassuming it could be. "You wake up one day, and it hits you that you aren't a young man anymore and you cannot do what young men do," he said.

"The things that were important at thirty-five are not as important at seventy," he said in a way that made me wonder whether he was talking to me or himself.

As he spoke, his face was like a map of the many places he'd been and full of impressions of the people he had seen along the way. I glanced at his worn, leathery hands, not unusual for a man of his age, periodically looking at my own hands, still smooth and relatively youthful. I listened to his low, gravely voice that had a Teddy Pendergrass ring to it, and reflected on the high tenor of my own.

"When I was your age, I worried about getting old," he said. "I started losing friends along the way, and at some point began to feel sorry for myself. I wrestled with the guilt of surviving combat tours where I'd seen younger men die, and my faith is what pushed me to be grateful for every day and take life as it comes. I'm grateful to be alive."

I asked him what his life is like being single in his seventies.

"Don't you get lonely?" I asked.

He paused, and his body language told me that he'd given much thought to this question. He never gave the impression that he wasn't satisfied with his life. "Since my divorce I had a few chances to get married, but I like my privacy, I like my space, I like my freedom," he said. "I don't like to feel obligated to anybody. Over the years when relationships got serious, in the back of my mind I knew that the relationship ultimately had an expiration date on it because I didn't want to go deeper into a commitment that required me to be something to someone I wasn't sure I really wanted to be. I cook for myself, and I travel alone. I enjoy my life and my charity work. I come and go as I please. I own my own home and it's everything I want it to be, and if I want company sometimes, I can have company. But for the most part, I enjoy living alone."

"Do you ever get lonely?"

"Yes." He responded without hesitation.

"So how you deal with that?" I said intently listening to his answer.

"At seventy, you just learn how to deal with it."

"What's sex like in your seventies?" I asked out of curiosity.

"It's good," he said with a smile, "although I don't need it as much as I needed it when I was your age. When I was your age I thought I would always need it. But I don't need it as much, and I'm okay with that. Your body changes in ways that you can't predict and so your mind just adjusts to it. It's frustrating for you now because, at thirty-five, you know, you have all your faculties and your body is very much intertwined with your sexuality. That's the way it should be, but it does change over time."

As I drove home that night, I thought about how affirming and frightening it was to know that much of his life reflected my own. I looked at him and saw myself. I live alone, and go and come as I please. I'm a great cook, and wash my own clothes. I take care of my house, and provide for all my needs. But that conversation with Mr. Penworthy troubled me for weeks because I realized that while I could live that way if I chose to, I wasn't sure I wanted to. It seemed a perfectly fine life for him. I just didn't know if I wanted it for me. I wasn't sure I wanted to be a man living without love when I get to be his age.

I wrestled with haunting questions like: What will become of my life? What about tomorrow? And what about love?

AFTERWORD

Shining on My Face

I heard a loud boom and was thrown about fifteen feet into the air before I realized the building had exploded. The wind brushed my face as gravity pulled me back down toward the pavement. The searing pain in my back was what I imagined it felt like to be shot. In midair I concluded no one was going to catch me, and I was going to hit the ground hard. There was nothing left to do but fall. It matters how you fall, because it can determine how you get up again—if you get up at all. I shifted my body so that I would fall on my left side. Being right handed, I figured if I couldn't avoid the fall, I would try to limit the damage to my left side. My left arm hit the ground first, then my head. I lay there with my sweaty face pressed against the hard earth, breathing into the dust. Luckily, the arm hurt worse than my head. But the sun was shining on my face, and I knew I was still alive.

I performed a quick mental diagnostic. I knew my name, where I lived, and where I was. Then I started a body check beginning with my legs. I needed to make sure they were working. I made two fists. They were a little sore, but I still had ten moving fingers. I rolled over slowly onto my back feeling the intense pain. I looked at my clothes covered with dirt, as if I'd rolled down a hill. But I was alive and the sun was shining on my face.

I laid still and closed my eyes. The sun was so bright that I was baking under its glare. I was surprised that after such a big explosion no one had rushed to help me. It was quiet, and I couldn't hear anything. I was alone. I knew I was going to be okay, I just didn't know when or how. I decided being on the ground wasn't so bad. We all get knocked to the ground sometimes. I had questions; I wanted to walk again but if I did would I get knocked down again? For a while, I didn't want to get up. I was hurting in so many ways that I couldn't even understand. However the ground is no place to live. Finally, I decided I could get up and walk again.

I wrestled with why this had happened to me until I finally stopped feeling sorry for myself and decided I wouldn't ask any more questions of God or myself that couldn't be answered. God is not always in our answers. God lives in our questions. I sat up, dazed and confused. If I were able to muster the strength to move on I would have more days, encounter new questions, and find new understandings of God. Turning around, I still couldn't understand what had actually happened or what was going to happen next. There was so much damage that I couldn't make sense of it all. But I lived through it and the sun was shining on my face.

As I looked out over the debris, I saw someone moving in the rubble. There was a knowing about Him as if He had all the answers to all my questions. Rummaging through the broken pieces of brick and mortar, it was as if He understood things about my past I'd never been able to comprehend. He stopped and with that look of satisfaction that comes when you've found what you're looking for, He stooped down and lifted a broken piece of brick from the ground. He blew on it and dusted it off. He continued searching until He found the other missing pieces of the brick and then, piece by piece, brick by brick, He put the building back together again. And as I watched Him work, I felt the sun shining on my face.

Contact Patrick D. Shaffer

General Inquiries: info@patrickdshaffer.com

Media Inquiries: pr@patrickdshaffer.com

Phone: 312.330.4405

Twitter: @patrickdshaffer

Join the Love Again FanPage on **Facebook**

Please visit my website: www.patrickdshaffer.com

Mailing Address:
1448 E. 52nd Suite #422
Chicago, IL 60615